God's Mission Vision

Pray, Go, Sow, Grow Love

Genesis 3:12; Matt. 28:19, 20; Rev. 7:9

John DeVries

With Todd VanEk and David Stravers

Published by Ephesians 3:20 Publishing
a division of Reaching America Ministries
4180 44th SE
Grand Rapids, MI 49512

ISBN: 978-0-9884202-7-4

Cover design by Michael Lautenbach

Printed in the U.S.A.

From the Author

Satan's most effective tool is to get us to follow our concept of good in place of God's concept of good. We sin when our concept of good pushes God's concept of good aside. Eve's desire to eat of the tree was good in her mind, and yet, because it was contrary to God's command, it brought sin to the entire human race. When the good that we want to do replaces the good God calls us to do, we lapse into sin. In doing so, we put ourselves in God's place. Does your concept of good in your Mission Vision match God's concept of good in his Mission Vision? We pray that God's Mission Vision is your Mission Vision, and that this little book will help you see if your Mission Vision matches God's. Each of the first fourteen chapters explores one of the ways God's Mission Vision can be described; the final five chapters deal with the way in which Mission India is putting God's Mission Vision to work.

-John DeVries

Dedication

For without their love, support, counsel, prayers and work, Mission India would not exist.

To my beloved wife, Adelaide.

To Able H. and Ken H. for a lifetime of friendship and commitment to India.

To Chirie and Kamala, who have shared the vision of the map of India lit up with the light of the gospel in every state, and for their creative application of the principles found in this book.

To Nancy, Jo, and the two Bills, who helped to launch Mission India.

To Deb, Cheryl, Tammy, and Dave B. who have worked so many years for Mission India.

To Gene, Neil, and Dave who were the first very able directors of Mission India.

To Don C., who brought focus to Mission India.

To Sid and Josh, through whom God has communicated the challenge of India.

To the entire MI staff both in the United States and in India for their tireless work.

To Dave Stravers and Todd VanEk—two very gifted Presidents.

Table of Contents

Part II- Mission India's Practice of God's Mission Vision

Preface

A little over fifteen years ago, Mission India offered me a free trip to India, and it cost me my life! Little did I dream at that time that I would someday be president of one of the most effective and efficient missions in the world. Mission India reports that our Indian partners (some 1,500 Indian missions) reach one and a half million persons with the gospel each year and see them become new believers as a direct result of the Spirit's working through one of our three training programs.

Twenty-five hundred church planters are being trained annually, five million boys and girls are being impacted through our two-week Bible Clubs every summer, and nearly 500,000 illiterate people have become literate and have started businesses that increase their income by an average of 55%. That isn't even the greatest result. These Indian missions are starting about 10,000 new churches per year, and each of those is reproducing new churches. These churches are bringing the good news to the largest unreached nation on earth, a place where one out of every six people in the world lives.

In this book, John DeVries looks back over his life and traces God's hand in developing a godly Mission Vision that still guides Mission India (MI) today. This book warns against substituting our concept of Mission Vision for God's concept. The book not only outlines major events in the history of Mission India, but it also develops the principles that are Mission India's foundation. I highly recommend this book for all who want to see kingdom expansion be the legacy of their lives.

Todd Van Ek, President, Mission India

Introduction

God's timing is not our timing, but it is hard to imagine that the Second Coming of our Lord will not come sometime soon, that is, before the end of the current century, not to mention the current millennium. What is delaying him? India! India is delaying him. We have not yet achieved God's objective that we make disciples of all people groups (nations). We are not even close. With more than one third of all nations unreached, and with nearly half of all individual people still unreached, India is the last greatest mission field.

It is no accident that before the year 2000, India was practically out of sight and out of mind for most Christians living in the West; India has now taken center stage in the world's thinking. Secular observers can list the reasons for this: India's dynamic economy, changing politics, expertise in communication technology, nuclear dangers on the Indo-Pakistan border, emigration of prominent Indians to Western countries, close relationships with Muslims in the Middle East and Central Asia, and India's developing political relationships to the other geo-political powers, United States, Russia, and China. Try finding a reference to India in *The Wall Street Journal*s of the 1990's, and you will search a long time. Pick up any *Wall Street Journal* today, and you will find India mentioned on page 1 or 2.

Believers know that this is not an accident of history. India is changing in even more profound ways, not least because the people of India are open to Christ as never before in history. The evidence is gathering to support the idea that an even greater movement for Christ in India during the 21st century could eclipse the great movements for Christ of the 20th century that occurred in China, Africa, Brazil, and Latin America. From there, perhaps it will expand into Satan's last defensive citadels in North Africa, Central Asia, and the Middle East, where people will never be open to the witness of Western infidels, tainted as they are by cultural and political prejudices. However, Indians, the most numerous and best-known foreigners in these regions, do not carry such stigma. Dare we dream of the day when God will use Indian believers to foment great movements for Christ in the most resistant nations on earth?

For Mission India, the decade of the aughts was a time for growth and expansion on the firm foundation of sound ministry principles and God-given focus. Many of the key teachings of John DeVries, as expounded in this book, were compelling reasons for me to leave an organization that had ministry to fifty countries to join a ministry to one country. Coming to Mission India in 2004, I was overjoyed to find a focus on the heart of the Great Commission – multiplying cells among specific people groups within specific communities. I was also impressed to find principles of ministry that too few mission agencies seem to understand, principles that are critical to transforming the Great Commission into the Great Completion.

Not the least of these was the successful transition of Mission India's India-side organization into a 100% indigenous-led, indigenous-staffed, and indigenous-motivated ministry. Chiranjeevi and Kamala, and those they recruited to help them, were totally responsible for implementing and incarnating the principles of ministry that John DeVries had learned through the years. Sometimes these incarnations took forms that we Americans could not understand, or perhaps even agree with.

Here is an example: If the focus of the Great Commission is church planting (not the salvation of isolated individuals), why would we invest resources in Children's Bible Clubs (CBC's)? I had asked John DeVries this question back in 1996, and I don't remember his answer, but I just didn't get it. Not until I started visiting Children's Bible Clubs in 2004, did I realize why Chiranjeevi had elevated this program, making it Mission India's top priority for funding and execution. There was great celebration when the number of children reached during the year hit one million. Wow, one million is a lot of kids to be hearing the gospel for the first time! Before the decade was out, five million children were being reached every single year, and the number of new believers was usually more than one million, and somethings as high as two million.

However, these big numbers were not the reason I was so impressed. In November 2004, I had latched onto another group of travelers that included Gene Davis and a representative of the Harry J. Lloyd Trust. We visited one of the worst slums in Hyderabad, stepping over the open sewers, squeezing between dilapidated "houses" constructed of cardboard and plywood, and ducking our heads to avoid scraping the low hanging electric wires. Coming to a small open area, we saw the 40 children lined up to greet us. They had been meeting in the daily after-school club for about three months, and they were eager to demonstrate what they had learned. There were no chairs, so we stood facing the children who were sitting cross-legged on the ground. Of course, we attracted a lot of attention, so many of the slum dwellers also gathered around.

One after another, children stood up to recite their memory verses, often entire chapters from the Gospels or the Psalms. They sang gospel action songs, performing the actions with beautiful smiles and great enthusiasm. Several of them gave personal testimonies.

One little boy stood up to answer the question, "Why do you like the Bible Club?" According to my translator, he replied, "I really like the games. We get to play cricket every Saturday. And I like the stories." At this point, my translator pointed to a very short woman standing next to me. "This lady is that boy's mother," he said. I noticed that she had the marks of Hindu temple worship on her forehead – three horizontal orange stripes, obviously freshly painted – so I asked her, "What do you think of this Bible club?"

"Oh, we like it!" she said. I said, "You know this is a Christian club, so why do you like it?" "Well," she said, "my son is doing better in school, he is now minding his manners, and he is teaching us to pray to Jesus." "Praying to Jesus?" I asked. "Are you Christians." "Oh no, sir," she replied, "we are Hindus."

Afterward, I asked the club leader, an energetic woman who reminded me of my fifth grade Sunday School teacher, "What about that family of the boy who gave his testimony? They are Hindus, but the lady said that he is teaching them to pray to Jesus?"

This is how she answered: "Yes, we know that family well. We visit them. They live in a one-room shack. Their house has only three walls; the fourth wall is just a piece of hanging burlap to give them some privacy. Their house has four Hindu idols, one in each corner. But as you said, their son is teaching them to pray to Jesus." At this point, the club leader grabbed my arm and looked me in the eye, "Did you know that Jesus answers prayer?" "Yes," I replied, "I heard that." Then, she said, "Don't you think that they will notice? Come back here in three months and they will be in our church. We have many other families in our church that came to know Jesus through their children."

Multiply this experience by a thousand, by a million, and you get a sense of what God is doing when mission happens his way. *Let the children come to me…Whoever does not receive the kingdom like a little child shall not enter it* (Jesus in Luke 18:16-17). Shortly after this event, we counted the adults who had come to know Jesus through the children, and in just one year, we found more than 80,000 adult converts, primarily parents, but also many other adults in the neighborhoods of Children's Bible Clubs.

Therefore, Mission India decided to invest at least 40% of its resources in Children's Bible Clubs. Mission India decided to limit its India activity to three programs: Children's Bible Clubs, Adult Literacy training, and Church Planter training. All three of these programs have their focus and purpose in planting and multiplying cells of new disciples.

Mission India invested significant resources in the measurement and oversight of these programs. Indigenous staff grew from about 60 people in 2000 to nearly 500 staff by 2010. More than 2/3 of these staff people live scattered throughout all the states of India, with the assignment to visit personally each of the 12,000 locations of ministry that are functioning at any given time. They give encouragement, confirm reports, monitor resources, mentor, and gather stories of God's miracles.

Mission India decided to prevent dependency on foreign funding by strictly limiting financial help. Some workers received scholarships or transportation expenses, but no evangelist, church planter, club leader, or teacher received more than one year of assistance.

Mission India decided to saturate India with gospel activity. It would have been easiest to work in the southern states of Tamil Nadu and Kerala, where more than half of the Christians in India live. Mission India could easily have invested all of its resources in these two states and could have seen great results. However, our indigenous leaders were passionate about reaching the entire country, so MI designated its resources based on population; this meant that the most heavily populated northern states, also the most Hindu, the most Muslim and the most unfriendly to the gospel, received the most resources.

Mission India decided to prioritize reaching people who were "culturally near" existing believers. Every member of every new church had opportunities to witness, and Mission India supported them with Scriptures, materials, training, organization, and accountability tools. As a result, these new churches became passionately committed to reaching everyone, and they assigned many of their workers to cross-cultural boundaries, to work in strange languages, among people of strange customs. God directed them, not because Mission India had targeted unreached people groups, but because the Holy Spirit moved them to go to the most hopelessly neglected. We sowed the seeds of the gospel in the fields, not in the barns.

Mission India collected the stories of miracles of transformation, shared this good news with the folks back home, and trusted God to motivate new partners, new money, and new prayers. In the summer of 2005, we reserved 25 rooms at the Grand Hotel on Mackinac Island, invited our most loyal donor partners, and for two days shared with them what God was doing in India. People got excited. The Lord touched their hearts. They prayed with more passion. They gave with more generosity. And, God blessed them when they gave.

We repeated this experience every year in the subsequent decade, and Mission India grew. We were able to invest $5 million in Scriptures and training during 2005. By 2010, MI's annual investments had grown to $10 million. We recruited thousands of new donor partners. New board members representing new regions and new denominations of America greatly blessed MI by their contributions. We forged a strategic partnership with The Bible League of Canada, which is now conducting all of their India ministries through Mission India offices.

However, even greater miracles occurred. The big miracle is that Mission India programs enabled ministry partners in India to grow to new levels of accomplishment. The year 2000 saw 644 new churches established. By 2016, this number had soared to 11,706 new churches in one year, and it is still growing. Not only this, but Mission India took its mission statement very seriously, "To help Indian Christians plant multiplying churches." Multiplication is important, because we can never fully reach India if new churches are not self-multiplying. Because we were determined to avoid dependency, Mission India did not help workers or churches beyond their first year of ministry. For this reason, we did not have systematic evidence that the newly planted churches were actually multiplying.

To remedy this, in 2007, we hired a third-party research firm to investigate. A randomized study investigated the new churches with several key questions in mind: Do the new churches exist after three years? Are the new churches planting additional churches? Do the churches continue to grow in members? Are they self-supporting? Are the newly trained church planters still in ministry? The results were astounding. We discovered that after 3-5 years, about 15% of the new congregations had died. At the same time, the surviving congregations had grown, on average, more than three times over in numbers of new churches, 80% of church planters continued in ministry, and the number of disciple-members continued to grow and multiply.

Mission India's 21st century has surprised us with the fulfillment of Paul's promise of incomprehensible divine power. Ephesians 3:20, the verse that promises that God "is able to do far more abundantly than all that we can ask or think," has become a daily reality. Therefore, we are asking, and thinking, and praying, and planning in bigger and bigger ways. We are encouraging one another with our Big Holy Audacious Goal (BHAG) "to see lives change, now and forever, by establishing a church in every village, urban neighborhood, and community in India." That goal is so big, we do not even know its number; at least 500,000 new churches are needed, perhaps a million. We must not cluster these churches together for mutual support and comfort, but we must scatter them throughout the primarily Hindu and Muslim neighborhoods of what is becoming the most populous and fastest growing nation on earth.

There are many reasons to doubt our own sanity. There are even more reasons to believe that we cannot even imagine everything that God is doing. "Transformation" has become a key term for us, partly because we know that holistic, spiritual, physical, and social change is what the kingdom of God is all about; partly because we are seeing miraculous change everywhere we turn in India.

The seeds of transformation work their way into the lives of Hindus and Muslims when they hear about the Great Healer and experience a miracle of physical healing. More than 90% of the testimonies we hear from new disciples begin with a healing miracle. Have you ever met someone who successfully committed suicide? I have. She was raised from the dead through the faithful work of a church planter in training. Being released from illness, hopelessness and death is happening not only to individuals, but also to families and entire communities.

During one visit to India, Josh Visser, Mission India's Director of Communication, found himself traveling in the tribal belt of southern Rajasthan, the western-most state of India that borders Pakistan and the Indian Ocean. Along with several Indian workers, he had turned off the highway and onto a small dirt road; they began slowly winding their way back into the hills. Eventually, they ended up at a church in a small country village. Pastor Karsenbai greeted them, invited them into his spacious church building, offered tea, and began to share how God was blessing him and his village.

During the conversation, Josh had the eerie sensation that he had met this man before; somehow he seemed familiar to him. Josh asked the pastor, "Have we ever met before?" Karsenbai looked at Josh closely and said, "Yes, I think I met you seven years ago. You were much younger then. I was too. I was only a student back then." Seven years earlier, Josh had taken his very first trip to Rajasthan, and Karsenbai was just finishing his one-year training course as a church planter.

When Josh got home from that trip, he dug through his old trip photos. Sure enough, he found some photos and notes that he had taken seven years earlier. A younger Karsenbai was one of the students he had interviewed at that time. Karsenbai had taken Josh to the village where he had begun his evangelistic work. Josh recognized his face in the photos, but looking at the background and the scenery around him, Josh could not recognize anything else. "Were these photos taken in a different place," he wondered? No, Josh's notes were clear—it was the same village, but it was so different in appearance from the village he had just visited.

Josh remembered that first long, hot walk to get to the village. There was no road back then, so he trudged up and down the barren hills on a dusty footpath, a blazing sun beating down, and no human habitations in sight. When Josh finally reached the village that first time, he found a small, dilapidated building that was serving as Karsenbai's home. It doubled as a tiny place of worship. Josh spent a Sunday morning there, worshipping with a couple dozen new believers. He remembered being struck by two contradictory thoughts: how great it was to see the first fruits of the gospel, and how difficult it was to imagine the life of this poor church planter, stuck out in the middle of nowhere in a place so desolate that you had to walk for hours to get there.

Fast-forward seven years. Karsenbai's worship building is now an impressive concrete structure where more than 300 newly born-again worshippers gather every Sunday, where children gather for Sunday school, and where meetings for prayer and Bible study minister to the village residents. Five nights a week, Karsenbai offers the use of the church veranda for an adult literacy class where 30 illiterate men and women are learning to read and write. One of his church members is the literacy teacher. It's an outreach program, and many of the students have already professed Christ. They will soon join the church.

Not only is the church growing, but the village, too, is being transformed. The new dirt road might not look like much, but it *is* much, considering what it was seven years earlier. No more long foot hikes to the main highway. In the last two years, Karsenbai and another pastor worked hard to get a new road graded into the hillside. They even invested more than 35,000 rupees ($550—more than a year's wages for the average villager) of their own money to rent equipment, with help from church members, they did much of the work of building the road themselves. Once the road came, electricity soon followed.

We dream big dreams, but God's dreams are bigger. God dreams of the day when His kingdom will transform individuals, families, and entire communities, not only by bringing them roads and electric power, but also by so much more than that. He brings them fullness of life—physical, spiritual and social transformation that is more than they ever imagined. When you bring Christ to a place, all the other blessings of the kingdom of God will follow. Whatever you pray for, God is likely to surprise you with even more!

How do you measure that? How do you measure what the Holy Spirit does through the years that follow our evangelistic investments of time and resources? Every year we at Mission India add up our numbers of new converts and new churches – but we also have learned to trust God to come alongside and start **multiplying** blessings of transformation in ways that are beyond our ability to plan or imagine! Stories like Karsenbai's continue to unfold all over India!

David Stravers, President Mission India, 2004-2014

Chapter One: Introducing God's Mission Vision

***Satan's great tool is to get us to do the good we want to do in place of the good
God has called us to do.***

People will benefit far more from what God wants to give them than from our best plans. Have you been shortchanging the people around you by merely giving them your plans instead of God's.

(*Experiencing God Day-by-Day,* pg. 107, H. Blackaby)

"I want to warn you, my friend said, "India is an experience. It will change your life more than any other country we will visit on this trip." His prediction was so true! It was my first overseas trip to Asia. Japan, Hong Kong, Taiwan, the Philippines, Sri Lanka—we visited them all, and that is just what they were, visits.

India was an *experience*. Not a pleasant experience either. Heat, dirt, poverty, the stench of urine, the smell of curry powder mixed with exhaust, cows wandering everywhere through traffic, horns blowing, heat, beggars clutching your shirt sleeves and emotions, little children racing to be the first to pick up the fresh cow manure. One out of every six people on earth is jammed in a land area about one-third the size of the United States. There is nothing like India. It is an experience. As a former U.S. ambassador to India put it, "India is an assault on all your senses and the world's only functioning anarchy!"

My first exposure to India lasted only three days, but that was enough to make me pray, "God, let's get it straight! I'll go anywhere, but not here." I call it the Jonah prayer; we all pray it at some time. God answered by sending us (my wife and me) back just twelve months later, this time for a whole week!

God is on a mission. Jesus wants *his mission vision* to be *our mission vision.* His vision involves determination, focus, commitment, longing, and a driving urgency. Jesus' vision is for all to have a love for him and for the lost. Jesus' vision involves much more than the salvation of individuals; it is much greater than that. It involves the transformation of nations, including all the thousands of people groups, and tribes and languages (Revelation 5:9) that make up India. This vison is not individualistic; rather, it is the planting of clusters of believers throughout the people groups. Nothing, absolutely nothing, will ever stop him from carrying out this grand vision that in Christ all nations on earth will be blessed! Certainly, not one of his servants that prays a self-centered prayer as I did will be able to hinder God's will, by making his own selfish comfort the prayer's object!

God set a huge test before Abraham when he called him to sacrifice his own son. It was a test about God's mission and Abraham's obedience to God in fulfilling the test. After Abraham proved to God that he was willing to sacrifice his son, God responded by including him in his grand vision statement: . . . *and through your offspring all nations on earth will be blessed because you have obeyed me"* (Genesis 22:18). God does not respond positively to self-centered prayers like the one I uttered as I left India that first time. He has a mission! He does not need people whose personal comfort is more important to them than is his mission. Those he uses in carrying out his vision, he first tests, and the test is often severe. On that second trip to India, accompanied by my wife, it was not just the smells, the poverty, and the crowds that tested us; no, we were also caught up in three riots. Our test was nothing like the one God gave to Abraham, but it was very humbling for us who had left four little children at home and who didn't want to come to India in the first place.

Our first test occurred when a man laid down on the railroad tracks to stop our already slow-moving train. Hundreds of screaming Indians, demanding funds to support their local political party, besieged the train. They wanted a separate state. They were on a mission. They were passionate, determined and focused. That was 1971, and they finally won their own state in 2013! One overeager participant climbed up the side of the train and began poking at us with his umbrella. People pitched stones through the open windows. We knelt in prayer. In the darkness of the compartment, we prayed, and the train lurched forward and rolled away from the shouting crowd.

Later that day our car was stopped, rocked, and nearly overturned twice. Again, we seemed to be enveloped by crowds of screaming Indians. It was hardly a hospitable welcome. I remember praying again, saying this time: "Lord, why are you letting all this go on? Why don't you do something for this country? Look at the filth, the poverty, the disorganization. Look at all the people. Are you blind to it, God? Do something, Father!" As I cried this prayer, I clearly sensed God speaking to me, saying, "I think I have done something for this country. What is it?" Quietly, with great embarrassment, I prayed, "Yes, you gave your Son for these nations of India!" "And what have you given for them?" He seemed to ask. "Not very much," was my immediate reply.

Then I knew. God was speaking and calling us to his mission. My wife and I were to give ourselves for India, to focus on India, to be passionate about India. God, in his grace and mercy, gave me a picture. I saw a very dark black map. It was a black map of India, and out of the blackness, little pin pricks of light started to emerge. The longer I looked, the more lights went on, until little shining lights lit the entire map. This vision was certainly not my vision born out of a romanticized love for India. Instead, it was a Spirt-given resolution that resulted in my collapsing in tears many times, alone in hotel rooms, praying for the land of India.

Having been called to be a worker in this field did not always result in joy. Our first ten years were marred with times of experiencing black depression and despair as I led others with me into the darkness of the slums of Bombay (now Mumbai). Yet the Lord never failed to lift us up out of the pit of despair and back onto the sunshine ladder of exultation that came from seeing lives transformed and hearing the joy-filled testimonies of new believers.

In the midst of the darkness, my wife and I began to experience a strange and unusual joy creeping into our lives – growing quietly, softly, powerfully, and unexpectedly. I remember Pastor Simpson crying and then apologizing as he prayed with a group of American pastors. The devil had attacked him during prayer, reminding him that he was an untouchable. How could he, an untouchable, be worthy to pray with American pastors? Then the Spirit came and reminded him that we are all equally children of the King. His tears were joyful tears. Little did I realize that day, how many tears there would be – tears of joy at the amazing mission of the Father, and our privilege to be a part of it.

God's vision is one of eternal, unlimited, awesome joy. It is sharing the joy of the Trinity. This joy caused the Father, Son and Holy Spirit to call us to join in their eternal dance of joy. On each trip to India, I have watched the little children who have met Jesus in the Children's Bible Club dance and skip in that same dance of eternal joy. They have been transformed and set free!

The triune God is on a MISSION to every nation on earth. *Then Jesus came to them and said, "All authority in heaven and on earth has been given to me. Therefore, go and make disciples of all nations, baptizing them in the name of the Farther, and of the Son and of the Holy Spirit, and teaching them to obey everything I have commanded you"* (Matthew 28:18-20).

After this I looked, and there before me was a great multitude that no one could count, from every nation, tribe, people and language, standing before the throne and before the Lamb (Revelation 7:9). God's great MISSION is that all nations on earth be blessed, all tribes, all people, all languages. God made this promise to Abraham after he had passed the Isaac test: *and through your offspring all nations on earth will be blessed, because you obeyed me* (Genesis 22:18). The heart of God's mission, the target, is all tribes, peoples, and languages. It is not *nation* in a political sense. The mission of God is to bless all tribes, all people and all languages, in India, and, of course, in the entire world.

India is a nation of nations, of people groups (4,500), tribes and languages (1,600 major). The blessing of God on India is to allow his love to flow through the healing of broken relationships and the bringing together of all people in the form of loving clusters of believers.

After leading my first seminar in India, we were walking through the dirty streets of Calcutta. We held the seminar in one of the largest Christian missions in India, a place that fed 25,000 poor people daily. The mission was near the place where Mother Teresa was doing her wonderful work. As we walked those streets, my mentor (who had been in India for several years) shared that the mortality rate of Indian missionaries (those who gave up and quit because of burnout or disillusionment) was the highest in the world—50%. The cause for this startling statistic was that these missionaries gave in to Satan's greatest temptation *to do the good that God had not called them to do.* Are you confused? Let me explain. Too often, we want to do good as we see it. God calls us to do good as he sees it. If our vision is not his, the result, even though well-intentioned, will be burnout, discouragement, and a sense of futility, because all one can then see is the overwhelming need and how little progress is being made. We must seek *God's* Mission Vision and *his* mysterious ways of thinking and working; we cannot work in *our own* power. Only then, will God release his infinite power and bless our efforts.

God's vision blesses all peoples, tribes and tongues. What does *blessing* all nations, all peoples, all tribes and all languages mean? We find the answer in Ephesians 1:9-10 where Paul tells us that God's grand purpose or mission is ***to bring all things in heaven and on earth together under one head, even Christ.*** Jesus is at work to bring all languages, people groups, tribes and nations ***back together again***.

God's vision begins with just two persons whom he called disciples. Christ is very clear about the meaning of discipleship (John 13:34-35). It is a relationship. One person cannot be a disciple any more than one person alone can be married. Just as marriage occurs only with two people, so also discipleship only occurs with two (or more) believers. Humans are like train cars with a hitch on both ends, one connecting with God and the other connecting with other believers. This is God's great blessing, the blessing of being brought back together again in communities of love. God's blessing is connecting others with him and with each other. God's great vision always begins with a transforming relationship involving God, another believer, and you. It reflects the love of Jesus bonding a believers' community, a community of love for Jesus and for each other.

To *go into all the world and make disciples* means to bring people together in a community that is so brilliant, so desirable, so utterly transforming, so local, and so visible (John 13:33 ff.) that the love of Jesus flows through them, into tribes, and into people groups, and into all the languages so that the blessings of God abound. Love reigns. God's love puts us *back together again*.

Such a mission will explode spontaneously. It can never be forced on a people from the outside. The heart of the Great Commission is to *make disciples*, and everything must lead to that goal. Jesus' vision is the making of disciples everywhere…to the ends of the earth. We in the West fail to understand the meaning of discipleship; our hyper-individualistic culture works against it. We export our vision, instead of God's vision, in our mission. We wonder why it is that our mission fails; why isn't God blessing us? The answer is simple; he cannot. We are not sharing the same vision. We are doing the good that God has not called us to do! We are trying to save individuals, but we fail to make disciples.

Roland Allen expressed it in these words. "Even if the supply of men and funds from Western sources was unlimited and we cover the whole globe with an army of millions of foreign missionaries and establish stations thickly all over the world, the method would speedily reveal its weakness, as it is already beginning to reveal it. The mere fact that Christianity was propagated by such an army, established in foreign stations all over the world, would inevitably alienate the native populations who would see in it the growth of the domination of a foreign people." (*The Spontaneous Expansion of the Church*, Eerdmans Pub., Pg. 19)

In agreement with this statement, Mission India will not hire missionaries to go into India and plant churches in the traditional way. Mission India will not fund the building of churches. It is committed solely to the training of nationals and encouraging *them* to do the task of spreading the love of Jesus throughout their own villages. Mission India is imparting God's vision to them; it is a vision of spreading the love of Jesus through their concern for each other and for all in the village, in their own language, to the people of their own tribe or extended family and ultimately to the entire nation.

What is God's vision? It is stated here, inspired by the Holy Spirit and given to John in Revelation: *After this I looked, and there before me was a great multitude that no one could count, from every nation, tribe, people, and language, standing before the throne and before the lamb* (Revelation 7:9). This is God's Mission Vision. This is the good God sees. If we have anything less than this, our vision does not match his. *...and through your offspring (Abraham's), all nations on earth will be blessed* (Genesis 12:3)

Chapter Two: God's Mission Vision Is Prayer

We were traveling by boat down the canals of a tropical paradise called Kerala, a southern Indian state. We were throwing New Testaments up on the shore near each village we passed. We knew that this was not the way to be distributing Scripture. Nevertheless, the Indian leader assured us that after soaking these villages in prayer, he would come back in two to three months, and he would find a church based on the Word of God planted in each one!

When we got back to his mission, we found his youngest son sitting on a wall, facing a building that was under construction. We asked our Indian host why his son was not working. His reply shocked us. He assured us that Joseph was working! Prayer is the work of missions, and Joseph's task was to pray. He faced the building site for a new youth hostel. As long as he prayed, workers worked; when he stopped praying, workers started to quarrel and fight. It reminded us of Moses and the Midianites (Exodus 17:10-13).

On Sunday, we celebrated communion with the Indian leader's main church and closed the sacrament with an unusual prayer: "Lord, grant that when we gather around this table again we may not have so much left-over bread." We were impressed with the way prayer saturated this mission. In India, prayer is not an unusual occurrence, as we discovered in later years. Indians pray. Everyone in India prays to some god. However, none of their gods has power. Jesus does. When the power of Jesus is unleashed through prayer, it amazes people!

When we returned home, we challenged the Mission India board to hire a full-time intercessor, which, much to our delight, they did. From this, Mission India's Intercessor Program was born. There are now several thousand Intercessors. Prayer is the foundation upon which Mission India bases its work, and we saturate everything we do with prayer.

In order to see things God's way, prayer must saturate everything. In every challenge, prayer becomes a love relationship with our Savior in which we ask that his will be done. Our Lord seems to be begging us to ask our Father for our daily needs. He tells of the persistent widow who wore down the crooked judge by her constant repeated request. The purpose of the story is to encourage us *always to pray and not to give up* (Luke 18:1-5).

While on earth, Jesus never began his work with plans; he always began with prayer. Read Matthew 4:2. What did Jesus do to engage the devil? Did he rehearse a number of arguments? Did he plan a clever strategy? No, he spent forty days in intense prayer and fasting. Jesus sensed that a great confrontation was at hand, and so he prepared for it by seeking the will of his Father in heaven through prayer.

In Luke 6:12, we find Jesus spending an entire night in prayer, prior to calling the twelve disciples. The call of *those* twelve was astoundingly different from whom others would have called. The people Jesus called to be his disciples were, to put it mildly, not the ones most would think would be chosen for discipleship.

Jesus referred often to his death and resurrection. As the time drew near, Jesus sweat drops of blood as he prayerfully prepared for his coming trial and death. Because of his prayer, the Father enabled him to bear the horrible suffering and death that he faced for our sake.

Prayer is like sitting in God's lap, enjoying his love and the assurance that he will use us and work with us, but that this is *his* plan, not ours. It is *his* work, and he gives us the delight of seeing it unfold to an extent beyond anything we could ask or imagine (Ephesians 3:20).

Faith is the ability to see beyond what the mind sees. It is the ability to see God's way. God, through his Word and prayer, will open our eyes to see eternal things. He will touch our emotions with excited anticipation as we wait for the unfolding of his plan through us. It is by prayer that we express our constant dependence on Him.

Put another way, it is operating in the flow of God's sense and not on the basis of our sense. Prayer is seeing beyond anything that we in human strength can see. Paul put it this way: *Now unto him who is able to do immeasurably more than all we can ask or imagine* (Ephesians 3:20). God's vision is seeing ways of doing things beyond what we think we can do. We call the result of his vision *miracles*. Stories illustrating that God does things we cannot even ask or imagine fill the Old Testament. God doesn't think as we do, or work as we work. Isaiah said it this way: *As the heavens are higher than the earth, so are my ways higher than your ways and my thoughts than your thoughts* (Isaiah 55:9).

The assault on Jericho is a good example. The stone walls surrounding the city were six feet thick, up to twenty-six feet high, and they were mounted on a forty-six-foot high embankment. A twenty-seven-foot wide moat, which was nine feet deep surrounded the city. The inhabitants of the city were vicious pagans, devoted to child sacrifice. God's plan for the destruction of this citadel of immorality was to have his people walk around it once a day. On the seventh day, they were told to walk around the city seven times and to toot their horns seven times; then the walls would tumble down. God does not think like we think. He doesn't work like we work. Think of Moses, Gideon, David, Elijah; God did through them what they never could have asked or imagined.

I was a very, very tired young pastor. Back in the sixties, regardless of the size of the church, in our circles, the pastor had only a part-time secretary; the rest was up to him. Preach twice a Sunday (two different messages!), teach all the catechism classes, and the ladies aid, and the men's society, and lead the youth group…it makes me tired just to think about it.

I was leading the youth group. They and I were both about asleep; the boredom was contagious. I had to do something to get their attention, so I asked them if they believed in miracles; while they said that they did, they didn't come to attention. I asked them if they had ever seen a miracle, and still no attention! Then, without thinking and certainly without using common sense, I asked them if they would like to see a miracle. That did it—they woke up and asked what I had in mind. I didn't have *anything* in mind; I just wanted to get their attention.

I didn't know what to do, so I breathed a prayer, "God give me your plan. Get me out of this situation," and the idea of building a church in Taipei came to mind. Our missionary to Taiwan had recently challenged our church to do this. The young people wanted to know the cost of such an endeavor, and I replied, "$10,000." My annual salary was $7,200. Can you imagine challenging young people to raise more than the amount the church paid its senior pastor? That certainly qualifies as being beyond common sense. I told them to pray, ask God for the money, and then vote. I asked them to write "yes" or "no" on a piece of paper and hand it in. The "yes" vote was unanimous! They wanted to experience a miracle and do something beyond what common sense said was possible.

After voting, they asked, "What do we do now?" I replied, "How do I know? This is supposed to be a miracle, isn't it? I don't know how to do miracles. God does, and you just voted to let him do it through you!"

After discussion, they agreed to place a little plastic bank in the shape of a church in every home of the congregation. They promised the church families that they would call once a month to collect their loose change. After collecting the loose change the first month, it took two and a half hours to count the $2,500 they received. Within ten months, the youth had collected, not the $10,000 we had set as our goal, but $12,500. Not only that, but also every fund in the church received over its budgeted amount! What would $12,500 in 1960 dollars be worth today?

A few years later, we started to collect funds for Mission in India, (called *Bibles for India* in those days). We did it by challenging youth groups to raise ridiculous (beyond common sense) amounts of money for India. This method of funding became our first method of funding and produced not only tremendous amounts of money, but also tremendous, positive effects for those who engaged in it. People often ask me what we did to start Mission India, and my reply usually is: "We prayed and forsook common sense and plans and challenged young people to pray and ask God for a ridiculous amount of money."

The young people became supply-side missionaries, praying for and funding the work in India. They not only began to think outside the box, but they also prayed outside the box. Divine power flowed through them, enabling them to do something beyond anything they could ever ask or imagine. Far more benefits resulted than the mere raising of money.

- Parents were thrilled, and they, too, became involved. Keeping loose change was not a sacrifice for anyone. The adults were dumbfounded at the amounts the kids raised.
- Adults loved the calls by the young people, and it knit the adults and kids together in a unique way.
- It lifted awareness of missions to a new high.
- The adults were motivated to find out more about India and the need of spreading the gospel there, because their children were involved.

Twenty years later, we asked one of the Taiwan missionaries about the church our funds had built, and he told us that the denomination had built a high-rise on the site; they sold many of the apartments and used the second floor as an office and the ground floor as the church. The $12,500 had grown into a million-dollar investment in Taiwan.

A little denomination on the east coast challenged many of their youth groups to pray for funds to supply their North East India churches to reach 700,000 Meitei tribe families with Scriptures. It was so successful that more funds were raised than for any other projects, but considerable criticism arose among pastors and leaders. The mission board of the church sent out a two-page justification; in it, they mentioned the following criticisms they had received of the challenge given to the young people in the denomination.

- Young people do not realize what they are biting off.
- The program is too big for such a small denomination.
- The goals of the local churches are totally unrealistic.
- It will take more dedication than our kids have to get this job done.
- This program will surely rob other missionary giving.
- This program bypasses the Missionary Fellowship.

The Board of Missions of the Evangelical Congregational Church replied by listing many ways in which they had not only raised funds, but they also cited some of the tremendous benefits which flowed to the churches and the young people alike. In it, they admitted that the young people did not know what they were getting into. The letter to the churches went on to list 14 ways in which the Evangelical Congregational Churches had been blessed here at home. Here are just some of the 14 pastoral reactions to the challenge given to their young people.

- If we can raise this much MORE money (for missions), it proves that we are not really doing stewardship properly.
- No other phase of our ministry was hampered; in fact, our treasury has more money now than before we began the program.

- Some washed out, cleaned up, and stereotyped youth groups were revitalized.
- This program made our kids come alive (adults too!).
- Adults couldn't wait to greet the youth as they came by to collect funds. Pie, cookies, and candy always awaited the young people. Both age groups said that they could talk to each other now.
- Another church said that if we can raise this kind of money through the young people, let's keep on, and they took on the support of an additional missionary.

The mission board of the E.C. denomination started this report by asking: "How can a mission project overseas be a blessing (to our denomination) here at home?" It was obvious that in involving the young people of the denomination in the miracle of raising ridiculous amounts of money for Scripture, two things happened. Not only did their Indian brothers and sisters receive the desired Bible courses, but tremendous spiritual and financial benefits accrued at home as well.

Is your mission vision limited to thinking that only what you can plan and do in your own human strength is possible? ***Your mission vision probably is good, but is it the good that God is calling you to do, or is it merely the good you want to do***? Has your fascination with the good you can do limited your vision from seeing the good God can do through you?

Listening prayer is the act of putting prayer before your plans. We are not to plan first and then ask God to bless our plans, but we are to pray first, and then we are to plan based on what answers we received to our prayers. This requires listening to God. Listening prayer is very important when a group decision is called for. The pastor of a large church near Washington D.C. was intrigued with the potential of listening prayer and decided to introduce it in place of discussion at the annual congregational meeting. The pastor carefully prepared a presentation with all the information needed about each item on the agenda, along with appropriate Scripture, and then he asked for a period of silent prayer before they voted on each agenda item. He was amazed at the fresh sense of harmony that accompanied the counting of each unanimous vote.

This pastor decided to introduce listening prayer into district meetings that consisted of delegates from some 200 small churches of that denomination. The meetings changed from being mundane to being electrifying. Delegates who were used to leaving early now stayed until all sessions were completed. The real test of listening prayer came when the district of 200 small churches received the challenge to raise $1,000,000 for a special mission project. This request could have created a considerable discussion as delegates might have expressed reservation about their ability to come up with such a staggering amount. However, they decided not to put their objections first, but first to listen to what God was saying. After a lengthy period of silent prayer, each delegate wrote the amount they thought God was asking them to raise. The answer that God gave them, unanimously, was 6.1 million dollars. Each person had written down this amount without knowing what the others had turned in! Three years later, these 200 churches in the district raised that amount for their project!

Many churches limit God to what they can accomplish with their own abilities, and they become, stagnant. They lack God's Mission Vision, because they have substituted their own plans and mission vision for God's mission vision. In a meditation for October 19th on John 18:36, Oswald Chambers in *My Utmost for His Highest,* writes: "The great enemy of the Lord Jesus Christ in the present day is the conception of practical work that has not come from the New Testament, but from the systems of the world in which endless energy and activities are insisted upon, but no private life with God.

Chapter Three: God's Mission Vision Is <u>Going</u>

Christianity is a *going* religion. The center of Hinduism is India. Asia is the center of Buddhism. The center of Islam is the Middle East, especially Mecca. The center of Christianity is always on the move. God moved it out of Jerusalem almost immediately (Acts 8). From there it covered the Roman Empire and then moved on through Europe into America. Those of us who have lived through the end of the twentieth century, on into the twenty-first century have seen Christianity *go* from West to East and to the South. Africa, which was 1% Christian in 1900, now, in the twenty-first century, is 50% Christian! No other religion has had a similar record of accomplishment in *going* as has Christianity. This should not surprise us. From Abraham's call to go, to the picture of the fulfillment of the going (Revelation 7:9), Christianity is about reaching every nation with the good news.

Just as farmers *never plant seed in the barn***,** so mission work seldom happens within a church building. A young pastor received a call to lead a dying church. He said that he would accept the call if the elders would agree to host one community family each month for dinner in their homes. The elders said that to get out of church once a month was too much to ask of them, so the young man turned down the call, only to have it reinstated a month later. The elders had decided to get out of the church at least once a month, as the pastor asked, and to invite a community neighbor into their home for dinner. The pastor accepted the call, and within two years, that *dying* church was reborn; it started to grow and soon had over two hundred attending worship. God's Mission Vision is very simple; it involves getting out of the church building and into some mission field, just as farmers get out of their barns and into their fields in order to plant corn.

God's Mission Vision

Read the eighth chapter of Acts. This chapter tells about the intense persecution of the fast-growing new church. *On that day, a great persecution broke out against the church in Jerusalem, and all except the apostles were scattered throughout Judea and Samaria* (Acts 8:1). In a very short time, the church had grown to 5,000 (Acts 4:4). It seemed nothing could stop the church, even as persecution drove the believers out of Jerusalem. God was fulfilling his mission vision: *Those who had been scattered preached the word wherever they went* (Acts 8:4). God uses every means, even the work of the devil, to enact his mission vision *that his church must be a going church* in order that all nations on earth will be blessed. Christianity is always on the move.

There are many ways for churches to *go* out of their buildings to bring the gospel to inner city communities and around the globe. Good friends of mine founded a mission called, *His Place*, and targeted a rough, inner-city housing development. It was such a rough neighborhood that during the first month of one summer, they averaged fifteen police calls per week. A widow from a near-by church approached the team. She volunteered her help. They sent her back to her church with instructions to get a few of her friends to meet once a week to pray for the housing development. They could not use her church at the development, because it was too dangerous. She went back to her church and informed her widowed friends of the need for a prayer group, and a small group of women began to shine the spotlight of God's love on the housing development through their weekly prayer meeting. The police calls dwindled from fifteen per week to less than fifteen for the entire rest of the summer!

The presence of Christ is established through prayer, and that presence drives out evil, just as light destroys darkness and heat eliminates cold. Thus, as churches cover neighborhoods with prayer, they pray in the presence of Christ and turn on the *spiritual light and spiritual heat.* They go out, as did the widow and her friends, by means of prayer, to places they could not physically go.

There are many ways to *go*. The Robert Taylor Homes in Chicago was one of the worst slums in the nation in its day. Thankfully, they have been torn down, and the area has been cleaned up. Before the time of dismantling the high-rise apartment buildings, a group of Christians planted a church to minister to the needs of the people living in the complex. It was discouraging work. Seven churches in southern Chicago decided to hold a thirty-day prayer time targeting this complex. Through prayer, they left their church buildings and went out to the Robert Taylor homes, praying the presence of Jesus into these homes. The church members also went out by mail and sent letters to each apartment, offering their prayers and a Bible correspondence course. The church, meeting in the Robert Taylor Homes, said that the thirty days of prayer resulted in the quietest, least troubled time they had ever experienced in the homes.

The idea for *going out* to sow seed had a unique application. Back in the sixties, the Grand Rapids Bible Correspondence Institute solicited Christian professionals to send an invitation to study the Bible on their professional stationary to others in their same profession. Thus, doctors wrote to doctors and lawyers to lawyers, inviting them to enroll in a Bible course and giving their personal testimonies as motivation to enroll. The fact that this was a correspondence study and there was no immediate personal contact encouraged people to enroll. The fact that the invitation came from another local professional was also attractive. Many professionals responded to this fresh approach.

Even though my church was large by standards of the day, I wanted to build it bigger. God put an idea in my head: *You cannot build an ear of corn. All you can do is grow one. And when you do it the right way, with one seed, each of the two ears produced by the one seed will have 600 kernels.* God's church is a living organism. Living things can only be grown. No one can build a church; it can only be grown. Growing something requires going to a field where seeds can be planted and grown.

Why sow seed in the barn? Farmers do not sow seed in the barn! They *go and sow* in a field. God's Mission Vision began to form in my mind. We were acting as farmers, strange farmers who were sowing the seed in the barn, and not out on the field! We needed to teach the Bible to non-believers where they were, and they were not in church. No matter how hard we tried, we could not move the field into the church. How could members be motivated to sow seed outside the barn, i.e., get them out of the church building and into the field?

We made up little postcards that said, *We live in tense and troubled times. The Bible brings a message of hope and comfort. We invite you to enroll in a free Bible course. Just send in this enrollment card.* ***NO ONE WILL CALL ON YOU.*** That little phrase was the motivational key, both for our members and for the recipient of the card. Neither party had to talk to anyone. Church members were willing to hand out the cards, and those who received the invitation to study seemed willing to send in the card, as long as they had the assurance that no one would call on them.

I encouraged church members to slip a card under the underwear in a department store and run, so they didn't have to talk to anyone. Maybe someone would find the card and send it in even if the person who placed the card was long gone! With that little bit of humor, some of the congregation went to work. Of the 800-plus members, about 100 took the distribution of the enrollment cards seriously. Even with that limited participation, in the first three months, we had responses from 110 people requesting that we enroll them in the Bible course. That response grew to 500 enrollments in the first six months. The locations and types of people who responded were interesting. Among the enrollees were a poverty-stricken family in West Virginia and a Vietnamese girl in Saigon along with her two friends, both Catholic priests. A teenage girl in Roy, Idaho and families from Idaho to Pennsylvania also enrolled! We were going to places we had never heard of!

Within six months, our little correspondence school, which now had 500 students, saw some amazing spiritual results. An agnostic who delighted in degrading the local church and who lived near the church building quieted down after studying the course and changed his attitude. A woman who had not been in church for 19 years started attending again. A man, who had been dismissed from his church several years earlier, studied the course with his family and was re-admitted into the church.

Most of the enrollment cards were distributed by personal contact, in spite of my suggestion to use "the leave one and run" method. One of the members helped a stranded motorist in a western state and then encouraged him to enroll. Two months later, we received his request for a course.

We did not limit enrolling to personal contact. We went *out*. We advertised in the regional section of the TV guide and were amazed when 140 people responded and enrolled! About ten years later, we tried three ads in the India edition of the *English Reader's Digest* and were swamped with 50,000 responses! We went *out* to India! Thankfully, by that time, we were printing the courses and not merely reproducing them at the church; we also had help from another agency.

Our youth group came up with the idea of *going out* on a week-long bike trip, visiting little towns and villages and going from door-to-door offering the courses. This idea spread to other churches, and the participating groups were called YICA. The serious name was *Youth in Christian Action,* but more often, they called themselves *Young Idiots*

Cycling America. In a one-week trip, the average group would enroll about 1,000 new students. YICA spread, and many local churches in west Michigan and Illinois sponsored bike groups. Some of these groups have continued into the 21st century. Parents, who were transformed on the trips, encouraged their teens to go. Several churches rented booths at local and state fairs to offer the Bible courses. Another group of Chicago churches rented a booth at the Flower Show in McCormick Place for several years. The movement spread rapidly across the nation and to countries around the world. At the end of the seventies, clusters of churches in 133 U.S. cities had cooperative correspondence schools that distributed over one million courses. We found that personally enrolling relatives and friends continued to be a very effective method of reaching people. A local dentist, upon completing the course, requested that it be sent to his son in Ft. Knox and also to a special friend in Wyoming, MI. We were *going*! A significant percentage of the church was moving *out*.

The church in India dates back to the coming of St. Thomas, the doubting disciple. The Mar Thoma church was proud of the fact that their origin is traceable to one of the disciples, but they had never been a *going* church. Christianity in India was bound up in itself. It had become one of the thousands of minor castes. Yes, there were a few evangelists handing out Bible courses, and we supplied them with materials, but they were exceptions. The church remained **a *non-going*** church until the twenty-first century.

In an effort to get the church *going,* Mission India decided to offer a training ministry in church planting. Rather than doing direct evangelism, Mission India decided to follow Ephesians 4:ll and make its ministry that of church leadership training. Thus, the statistics that Mission India reports each year are the result of the Indian Christian Leadership implementing this training. The church members did the evangelism; Mission India did the training. We established a northern campus in Delhi and a southern one in what was Madras at that time. About twenty students enrolled in each place. It did not work. The grass-roots students returned home with their diplomas and with their pride. Since they had been to school in the big city, they felt themselves too good to go into the villages.

With the guidance of our director, Dr. Chiranjeevie, we decided to make local churches the campuses to train the pastors and their staffs to teach the members of their congregations to be church planters. We did clusters of twelve students per church, and we gave an annual living stipend to each student and small honorariums to the teachers. We divided the year into three semesters, each beginning in the local church building with one month of classroom teaching, followed by three months of *going* into the surrounding villages. A goal of *going out* to one thousand homes in the year was set, along with that of planting one new worship center. Churches started to *go;* they caught God's Mission Vision of *going.*

Mission India did not stop with training church planters. In India during the last three decades of the twentieth century, about 700 million people were either partially or fully illiterate. Headed by Dr. Kamala Chiranjeevie, Mission India developed Bible-based literacy primers and trained thousands of teachers in about 25 major languages. India churches have *gone out* and set up literacy classes and have graduated over half a million students! Student income goes up fifty seven percent during the year they are in the program, and it continues to rise after they complete the classes. The practices of hygiene taught in the classes result in increased good health. Each page of the four primers has a verse of Scripture that the students memorize.

The Indian churches are also trained and equipped to *go out* to the children, both in the ten-day summer program and in the year-round, after-school clubs in which much mentoring and teaching are given to the children. Six million children are reached each year by these programs, because the Indian churches have been challenged, trained, and equipped to *go out* to the children with new materials each year.

At this point in world history, the *going out* of the India church in Christ-ward movement may become the greatest religious movement in history as God's Mission Vision takes hold (cf. *Christianity Today*, Nov. 2017). Mission India is training the churches to *go* into the field and plant the seed of God's word. The *spiritual farmers* of India are going out to millions of boys and girls every year and planting the seed of eternal life in their hearts and minds. Indian Christians are going to thousands of illiterate adults each year, teaching them how to read God's Word and guiding them to understand its eternal, timeless, transforming truths.

Chapter Four: God's Mission Vision Is <u>Sowing</u>

God calls us to plant the seed of eternal life—God's Word, the Bible. *For you have been born again, not of perishable seed, but of imperishable, through the living and enduring Word of God* (1 Peter 1:23). Planting the seed is teaching the Bible to those who do not yet know Jesus. A farmer got a new irrigation system, and every day he went out to water his field. At harvest time there was nothing to harvest; he had become so engrossed in doing the "good" of watering and irrigating that he forgot the ultimate good. He forgot to plant the seed. That is the picture of many churches today; they become so engrossed in doing many different good things that the act of planting the seed of eternal life (teaching a simple overview of the Bible) throughout their neighborhoods is totally neglected. As happens to farmers who only irrigate fields and never sow seed, many churches, both in India and in the West, never grow.

The original Bible course we used was a four-booklet course called *The Bible's Answer*. By 1978, ten years after it was written, one million copies of the first booklet had been distributed. We sent it to India with high expectations of how it could be used there. It failed. People did not respond to it. Mission India also tried *Rebel with a Cause*, a course on the Gospel of Mark; *The Gospel of John,* a four-part course on the Gospel of John; and the *Touch of His Hand.* We tested these courses, and none of them was successful.

We had a twelve-lesson children's course—a little course that went from Genesis 1 to Revelation 21 in twelve lessons. It only took three days to write. It worked. This was it! In twenty years, by 1998, we had distributed nearly thirty million copies of this course in India, and adaptations of it were used in another 50 countries. This little course has been a model for other countries. We estimated that by the year 2000, nearly one hundred million courses like this were used throughout the world.

A parishioner asked if we had any copies of the course available in the United States, and he took about four hundred. He called about a year later and said that he had given all of them away. He invited us to come to a local restaurant. When we walked into the restaurant, the waitresses descended on him. I asked what was going on, and he said that he had started a Bible study with them using the *Guide to Happiness* course. One waitress had had cancer and now was cured. The others never understood the Bible, but now they did! He told of another Bible study he had started with six students from three Christian colleges in the city. When I expressed my skepticism, he said that even these college students didn't understand the flow of the Bible. The Bible remains a best seller in the United States, but it is seldom read, in spite of the fact that over 80% of the homes in the United States have at least one copy.

The Bible must be taught systematically, i.e., from creation to the second coming, just as this little *Guide to Happiness* course does. In India, because so many cannot read, they are taken through the Bible with pictures of creation, the fall, the crucifixion, the resurrection, and the ascension and return of Christ. We developed a colored picture flip chart that evangelists use to teach the course. This flip chart is printed in India. The Bible's message is taught to the illiterate masses through pictures. After completing this course, they are introduced to the Bible in the 12-lesson, *Guide to Happiness* Bible study course, read and taught to them by a local church planter. Finally, they study a Scripture compilation that spans creation to completion.

When commenting about the *Guide to Happiness* course, an Indian held up a glass of water, saying that the Hindu mind can be likened to a glass of water full of baffle plates. The goal is to get the gospel past the baffle plates into the soul (or bottom) of the glass. These *baffle plates* are religious concepts, and the Hindu mind has more baffle plates than any other religion. To have the Hindu understand the uniqueness of Christianity, one must get past all the baffle plates of heaven and hell and the Trinity, down to the person's soul. This is nearly impossible if one starts with the concepts of heaven and hell and Jesus' work on Calvary. This news is absorbed and quickly given a Hindu twist. The Hindu brags about worshipping 330 million gods, so it is very easy to add Jesus as the God of love.

He then held up the *Guide to Happiness* course and explained that its goal is to penetrate to the soul of a person with the gospel without being stopped by the baffle plates of the Hindu mind. This course starts with the teaching of creation and ends with the teaching of Christ's second return to earth; it does this in just twelve lessons. This is linear time, and the Hindu, who believes in reincarnation, has no beginning or end. His worldview is cyclical. Linear time and cyclical time are opposites. The Hindu just keeps on going around in an endless cycle of births, lives and deaths. Progress is replaced with fatalistic acceptance of one's current position. When the Bible is presented chronologically (linearly), from creation to Christ's second coming, linear time is introduced, and that is unacceptable to any believer in reincarnation. The Hindu may have 330 million gods, so the assimilation of another God, Jesus, into that pantheon is relatively simple, but he cannot assimilate a beginning and an end (linear view) into his cyclical worldview.

Thus, the seed of eternal life is planted in the soul of the Hindu; a Creator God exists who is Triune; God's Son paid for our sins, and, thus, made all who believe in Jesus Christ his Father's children. Someday, time will end, and he will come again to re-create and make all things new.

As we look at the world, do we see vast fields of lonely people, waiting to be bound together with the seed of eternal life? In India, the Bible is planted in the setting of little caring communities of people who are in the process of being spiritually and physically transformed. *For you have been born again, not of perishable seed, but of imperishable, through the living and enduring word of God* (I Peter 1:23).

Seeing the good as God sees it, not as we see it, means that we adopt a dramatically different way of looking at life. Transformation is born in, and grows out of, believers' communities where studying the Bible takes place. Lasting transformation is rooted in continuous Bible Study. God wants nothing less than complete transformation, spiritual and physical, flowing out of believers' communities. That transformation is not merely one of individuals, but also of communities, people groups, and tribes. As Peter wrote, we are born again of the imperishable seed of God's Word. **Failing to plant it is as ridiculous as being a seedless farmer**.

Practicing God's Vision is looking at life in terms of the good *God can do* and not limiting ourselves to what we can do. Put another way, it is operating in the flow of God's sense, and not on our common sense. This part of God's vision means seeing beyond anything that we can see with only our limited human vision. Can we make a kernel of corn mysteriously grow? We can plan. We can build. We cannot in our own power, germinate seed; we can only plant seed. Eugene Peterson, in *The Message*, paraphrases this by saying that God doesn't think as we do or work as we work. Isaiah said it this way: *As the heavens are higher than the earth, so are my ways higher than your ways and my thoughts than your thoughts* (Isaiah 55:9).

As we look at life, do we see fields, vast fields of lonely people, waiting to be bound together as the seed of eternal life, the Bible, is planted in the setting of small, caring cells of people? Seeing the good as God sees it, not as we see it, means that we adopt a dramatically different way of looking at life. Transformation is born in, and grows out of, believers' communities where studying the Bible takes place. Lasting transformation is rooted in continuous Bible Study. God wants nothing less than complete transformation, spiritual and physical, flowing out of believers' communities. As Peter wrote, *For you have been born again, not of perishable seed, but of imperishable through the living and enduring word of God* (I Peter 1:23).

God’s Mission Vision

Chapter Five: God's Mission Vision is <u>Growing</u>

It is through the multiplication of visible, accessible communities or cells that the gospel explodes and spreads. This process may be called *growing love* or *celling*. These cells spread like dandelions in a springtime lawn. Jesus defined *community* in terms of a relationship he called *discipleship*, suggesting that discipleship is having a love for each other that is so striking and fresh that unbelievers have the right to judge the reality of one's being a true follower of Christ by a person's display of it (John 13:35). The goal of Mission India is to have a transformational witnessing prayer cell in every village of India. Through these cells, the entire community is blessed. These cells are small, often consisting of only 10 or 20 people. They consist of transformed believers who are bonded by love and concern for each other and for their village. They are dynamos for all forms of transformation—from dads being set free from alcoholism to care for their families to the transformation of villages with paved roads and electricity. Most of all, members of these cells find a personal value and an acceptance they never had before. Such little believer cells or prayer cells multiply spontaneously.

These little communities of believers multiply wherever they are planted. One of these cells was started in a slum called the Black Hills in a midwestern Michigan city, and in just six weeks, it had spontaneously multiplied from the original one to four, covering six adjoining neighborhoods. Lonely people are hungry for fellowship and love. Fearful people search for peace. Here in this slum of a relatively small city, we found the same spontaneous response to small clusters of people gathered in concern, prayer and friendship as we experience in India. What would the United States be like if we began to *cell* our inner cities?

For most Western believers, the word *evangelism* means leading *an individual* to Christ and providing *eternal life insurance*. That is only half of God's vision! In the year 2000, Mission India stopped using the word *conversion* and started using the word *transformation*—transformation of personal lives, families and entire villages. The results exploded. God views conversion as a two-sided event: people are transformed to be in love with him and with each other! It is a transformation of relationships.

Building huge churches results in making the church a spiritual business that depends upon professional management; sometimes it fails to provide its members with community. God's great goal is to bring everything together under one Head (Jesus) in glorious community (Ephesians 1:10). Either God *grows* the church, or we *build* it in our own strength. Either a church is grown through the inner transformation of its members, bonding together in spiritual love, or it becomes a dead, unattractive organization, built like any business. A dynamic preacher may lead it, and its growth is fueled by human communication skills. It remains hidden in a building, and it does not spread. When the pastor leaves, its membership dwindles and the church dies. Growing loving communities is God's mission vision. Churches are living organisms. A true church can never be built. It can only be grown.

Today, in spite of increasingly intense persecution, these little transformational cells of Jesus followers are spreading and reproducing themselves in an unstoppable way across all of India (and China and elsewhere). They are meeting the peoples' deepest needs of acceptance and love, which is at the heart of all transformation. Growing love, expressed in these cells, brings heaven down to earth.

We can become so lopsided in our outreach that we begin to do the good God hasn't called us to do when we present accepting Jesus only in futuristic and individualistic terms. Jesus told us to make disciples. While that starts with eternal faith in his saving work, it also includes growing small, transformational cells which meet the needs of lonely people and become magnetic, drawing others in naturally. God sees community as the goal of salvation now, in time, and then in eternity. God's goal is to bring everything back together again! *And he made known to us the mystery of his will according to his good pleasure, which he purposed in Christ, to be put into effect when the times will have reached their fulfillment—to bring all things in heaven and on earth together under one head, even Christ* (Ephesians 1:9-10).

When we substitute our vision for God's vision, and substitute the good we want to do, for the good God calls us to do, Satan has tricked us and made us ineffective. God's vision is *celling*; the establishment of believers' cells or communities in every nation, tribe, people and language (Revelation 5:9; Matt. 28:29). *Celling* is forming witnessing prayer and Bible study cells in which believers are tied together by love for Jesus and for each other. The cell may grow into worshipping groups or churches, but these cells are local, accessible, visible, and inviting, and they spontaneously spread everywhere.

Using celling as our goal, we can measure progress by area and by people group. We can know where we are in the fulfillment of the Great Commission, and, therefore, know how far we have yet to go. What God is doing is not seen by the media or even by the average follower of Jesus in the United States. Nevertheless, it can be seen, and it can and is being measured. The results are startling! *What eye has not seen, nor ear has not heard, nor what has never entered into the heart of man, such are the things which God has revealed to those who love him* (1 Corinthians 2:9).

Through Abraham and his descendants, the blessing and love of the Father, expressed in Jesus Christ, will be planted in every people group. God repeats this promise throughout the Old Testament. In Psalm 22:27, the poet tells us that the ends of the earth will hear about God and be glad. This phrase, *the ends of the earth,* appears many times in Old Testament poetry and in the prophets, especially Isaiah. These are all references to the Abrahamic promise recorded in Genesis 12:1-3, namely, that every nation, people, tribe and language will know the love of God, and be blessed in Christ.

Matthew 24:14 tells us that only upon the fulfillment of this promise will Christ return: *And this gospel of the kingdom will be preached in the whole world as a testimony to all nations, and then the end will come.* This preaching of the gospel means more than handing out a few tracts; it means more than preaching on radio or TV. The gospel message is not fully grown until love *grows*, and this requires that there be both small, visible communities of love and transforming, divine power in every community. The gospel is not fully proclaimed until believers' communities are established in every people group, in such a way that all can see the amazing, transforming love and power of Christ. These believers' communities demonstrate the truth and power of God's Word. They express God's love by their mutual care and by God's transforming power. They bring relief from poverty and sickness. They set the prisoners free from the hopelessness of caste and reincarnation, which Gandhi described in his autobiography as being *a burden too great for any to bear.*

God does practice a type of universalism. No, not every individual will be saved. Many still will be lost. But, in glory there will be a multitude such as John saw: *After this I looked, and there before me was a great multitude that no one could count, from every nation, people, tribe, and language, standing before the throne and in front of the Lamb*

(Revelation 7:9). Every one of them will have believers' communities in them, so that all will be represented in glory.

The twentieth century has been a time of unprecedented explosion on all fronts, exploding birth rates and exploding discoveries in science and technology. Much of the world has moved from animal-driven locomotion to gasoline-driven, from ox carts to cars and tractors. Most of the nations of the world are electrified. Cell phones have linked the world together. When we began our mission in India, we had to book telephone calls, and often it took two or three days to get through. Today, calls are made from the United States to India as if the office in India were located next door. Birth rates have sky rocketed, adding more humans to the world's population than in the previous nineteen centuries combined.

If we could graph the growth of the world's population, it would take a piece of paper approximately six miles long to graph the rise in population from our ancestors to the first one billion people (1900). It would take only six inches to graph population growth from five to six billion, and only one inch or less to graph the rise in population from six to seven billion people! We live in a world of young people, childbearing young people. Few of us can comprehend the staggering number of people who will populate the world by the end of the 21st century. One out of every six persons currently lives in India; they will continue to populate that already-over-populated nation, where half the people are now under 25 years of age.

From God's perspective, there is an even more significant explosion. It is the change in the location of Christianity from West to South and East, which occurred during the second half of the twentieth century and is continuing now. In 1900, 70% of all Christians were located in Europe and North America. By 2000, just one century later, 70% of all Christians lived in South America, Africa, and China, leaving only about

30% living in the West. In the first years after Christ, there was one Christian for approximately every 360 non-Christians. That has changed dramatically in the twentieth century. The ratio today is one nominal Christian for every two non-Christians, and one evangelical believer for every seven non-believers. C. P. Wagner in, *The Crest of the Wave,* says that at the beginning of the twentieth century, approximately ten million Christians lived in Africa. Today, current statistics show half of Africa is Christian! The same thing has occurred in Latin and South America. China has had a five-thousand-year history as a non-Christian nation. Around 1949, the Protestant church in Africa numbered less than one million believers, and 90% of its funds flowed into the church from the West. The door to the West was slammed shut, and suddenly the church exploded. By the initial decade of the twenty-first century, the church had grown to an estimated 140 million believers. Northern China has literally become saturated with small believers' cells. God's Mission Vision is built on the transformation of individuals, transformation expressed in an active love for other believers. This love is public; it is not hidden in some building called a church.

What happened to China and Africa during the twentieth century is now happening to India during the twenty-first century, as illustrated in maps produced by the Southern Baptist World Mission Board. One map portrays in red dots the number of unreached India people groups at the beginning of the 21st century. Just fifteen years later, by 2015, the map had turned color, indicating that a large number of these unreached groups had heard the gospel, and up to two percent of them had already become believers, gathered in small believer communities.

Could it be that the church is exploding spontaneously, because two-thirds of the world still lives in communal societies and, thus, *cell* naturally? Christianity came to the Americas in the community of immigrants, and from there it was driven out into all parts of the world by a massive mission movement. This movement began shortly after the Second World War, and it was worldwide. While America was becoming increasingly individualistic, and Christian evangelism centered on individual salvation, Christianity was received differently throughout the people groups of the developing world. It was received communally. It exploded through nations that had not yet been poisoned by individualism. It exploded in nations where the people were still linked together in cells called *extended families*.

We must make a distinction between *lost* people and *unreached* people, as does the president of Mission India, Todd VanEk. The *lost* have heard about Jesus, some many times, and have yet to receive him. The *unreached* are those who have never heard of Jesus. We must target them first, without forgetting the lost that are still around us. The Western church spends approximately 86 cents of every dollar received on self-maintenance. It spends another 13 cents to reach the lost, many of whom have a daily opportunity to hear the Good News, but seldom see the transformation that occurs in small cells. That leaves two cents of every dollar available to complete the Great Commission by reaching the *unreached;* this would not be the case if the Western church had God's Mission Vision.

Father V. J. Donavan worked among the Masai tribe in Africa, teaching the Bible to them weekly for a year. He tells his story in an excellent book entitled, *Christianity Rediscovered.* After a year of weekly teaching the Bible to the Masai, he decided that some tribal members were ready for baptism, and he proposed that he baptize a select few. Some had missed many lessons. Others had been caught in immoral practices. These he would not baptize, a typical Western, individualistic decision. Donovan felt that they were not ready for baptism. However, the village leaders informed him that he would baptize all of them, or none of them.

"Why Father do you insist on breaking us apart? We are one. When a person did not come for Bible study, we as leaders took it to him. When they did wrong, we reprimanded them. You will baptize all of us, or none of us."

On page 88 of *Christianity Rediscovered,* Donovan makes this astute observation: "We had always looked at the Masai and said, 'It is the terrible indifference of the tribe that makes it so hard for an individual in it to be a Christian, the terrible inertia of the tribe. What chance does an individual have in such a setup?' Precisely that same inertia can turn into a dynamic vital force, enabling an individual to cast off his despairing, hopeless, futureless vision of the world, and share in community hope. I know many individuals who would never have been able to take that tremendous step on their own. In community, they have. In short, it is not possible or desirable to convert the Masai as individuals, but it is possible to evangelize them as groups."

If the West is going to return to Christ, it will happen only when Western Christians are converted from focusing on an exclusively individualist salvation to a *celling* or a community approach. Donovan puts it this way: "A missionary facing an alien pagan culture, to be an efficient instrument of the gospel, has to have the courage to cast off the idols of the tribe from which he came. There are many idols, but the two that I believe particularly mesmerize the Western church are individualism on the one hand, and love of organization on the other (*Christianity Rediscovered*, page 89).

Until Western Christians are willing to exchange their view of evangelism from being one of individual conversion to be God's view of developing small cells that publicly display Christ's supernatural love and, thus, bless all people in the neighborhood, the West will continue its precipitous slide into paganism. Jesus commanded us to make disciples, and disciples come in groups of two or more (John 13:33-35). Churches in every county need *to cell* their county. They must place prayer and Bible study cells in every neighborhood, every business and factory, and in every dorm and apartment building. These *cells* will sparkle with divine presence (Matt. 18:20) and will spontaneously spread throughout every county, just as they are now doing in India and in China. The West will see the same, exciting, miracle-filled spread of the gospel that we are seeing in India. And, these *cells* will be self-financing.

Bob and Betty Jacks wrote a book entitled, *Your Home, A Light House—Hosting an Evangelistic Bible Study*, and in it described the rapid spread of Bible study cells throughout Connecticut (Nav. Press). On page 25, they show a listing of how one home Bible study multiplied to eight new small groups, bringing 104 people to learn about the Lord!

The Triune God created us in his image, as relational beings to love—to love him, to love our neighbors, to love self, and to love his creation. Loneliness is our single greatest problem. To make disciples is to form cells of new believers in which the love of Christ is so evident that the unbelievers are given the right to judge the validity of the faith of the members of the cell by its presence among them (John 13:34). Jesus calls us to *celling,* or, to *make disciples*, as he described it.

God's Mission Vision

Chapter Six: God's Mission Vision Is Measurable

Does the time ever come when we can say, "We have completed the Great Commission in this nation or in this area, and it is now time to move on?" If we view the Great Commission purely in terms of winning individuals to Christ, then no one can ever give an adequate answer to the question of when the Commission is fulfilled. However, if we interpret the Great Commission to be creating transforming Christian communities (disciples) in every people group, we may be able to give some sort of answer.

We believe that a workable definition of the fulfillment of the Great Commission might be as follows: *A systematic, measurable, saturation of specific people groups within specific transformational geographic communities with multiplying cells in the body of Christ, which are accessible culturally and geographically to every member of the community.*

1. A Systematic

One of the great problems with missions is a lack of a systematic approach to a nation. The word *mission* covers a multitude of activities, and no one seems to have a clear goal. Without a clear goal, we cannot measure progress. Since there seems to be little consensus of where we should be fulfilling the Great Commission, there is a corresponding ambiguity in measuring how far we have come! If we take as our simple and clear understanding of the Great Commission to be growing love through the planting of clusters of committed Christians in every conceivable people group, then we have made significant steps toward being able systematically to measure the progress of fulfilling the Great Commission.

2. Measurable

The second key concept in the definition is the word *measurable*. One reason why the church is so disinterested in evangelism is the fact that there seems to be little measurable progress. Luke records the baptism of three thousand believers on the day of Pentecost; by doing this, he demonstrates that progress in spreading the gospel can, and should be, measured numerically. In Acts 4:4, he continues recording the spread of the gospel by recording that the church had grown to number five thousand men, or house churches. The measurement to be used to determine progress toward the fulfillment of the Great Commission is the number of cells planted within visible and accessible reach of its neighbors, and the corresponding number of unreached people groups that are saturated.

Mission India carefully tracks the location of its church planting classes each year, recording the place of all worshipping cells formed by each church planting student. Thus, the progress of the gospel's spread is carefully and systematically measured by state, district, village and people group in terms of prayer cells formed, literacy classes completed, and children's Bible and after-school clubs established. This information is placed on a map of India each year, pictorially telling the story of advancement toward completion of the Great Commission.

3. Saturation

Each mission should decide the *saturation* or fulfillment point. How many of these cells must there be per person? This will vary considerably depending upon the type of church planted, types of people groups, geography, village situation, neighborhood and languages. The saturation level must be determined for each district. These ten-year goals should then be added up to get a reasonable goal for the entire nation.

4. Of specific people groups

There are two concepts in this definition. We work with people groups and their geographic location. We believe that attempts to reach people groups apart from geographic locations are unrealistic. We must always speak of the people groups within a specific village or community. The Great Commission is fulfilled, in a specific geographic area, when all the identifiable people groups within that area are saturated with *multiplying cells in the body of Christ.*

5. With multiplying cells in the body of Christ

Christ's command is to make disciples. He gave a model of discipling with his own band of twelve disciples. Disciples are found in small clusters of believers, linked together by the new love that they have found in Christ. This new, sacrificial love and the resulting relationships are so striking, so different, and so attractive that the non-Christian, observing how the Christians live, are given the right to judge the reality of their faith on the basis of the demonstration or absence of this love (John 13:33-35).

The essence of Christianity is the community of believers who are practicing the new love of Christ in their relationships with each other. They come together regularly for worship and praise, and while this is essential to their nature, it is not the unique point which sets them apart from other religions. What does set them apart is the love they show for each other which makes them different from any other group in society. Christianity cannot be a privatized religion, such as the other religions of the world. Making disciples is always a matter of two or more people showing dramatic, new concerns for each other and for their neighborhoods. These cells are not only to be self-guided and self-financing, but they are to be self-reproducing. The new disciples not only demonstrate love for each other, but they also demonstrate a practical love for *all* people, and out of that love, new, small communities of believers are formed.

6. *Which are accessible, culturally and geographically to every community member.*

The small cells of transformed believers are planted publicly. The villagers know about them, for they see them in operation each day. The cells are accessible, because they are present in the village. They are accessible geographically. They are also accessible in terms of the people group to which each person in the village belongs. Each person sees *his own kind* of person demonstrating this unique love and care.

We must never underestimate the power of these small cells of believers in reaching the lost for Christ. Michael Green, in his excellent book on evangelism, *Evangelism in the Early Church*, points out the incredible obstacles to the spread of the gospel faced in the New Testament period, both in the Roman and in the Jewish world. The only thing that could overcome those obstacles to the spread of Christianity was the evident, demonstrable love displayed by the new Christians.

These Jesus cells are now beginning to blossom all over India! They show that Christianity is not a private religion, consisting of personal devotions during the week and attendance at a religious meeting on Sunday. Christianity is a sacrificial commitment of one's life, not only to Christ, but also to other believers and to non-Christians alike. These small clusters of disciples, demonstrating their new love for the Savior and for all his people, form the basic attraction point that will pull all of India into the transforming presence of the true God.

God's Mission Vision is Measurable

If we view the fulfillment of the Great Commission *not only as the salvation of isolated individuals,* but also as the *systematic and measurable planting of cells of disciples in every area* among every people group, we will have arrived at a definition of the Great Commission that can be systematically measured and accomplished. Many Christians in India have adopted this definition of the Great Commission and are working together, area by area, to saturate the second largest nation on earth with clusters of believers living in dramatic, winsome, and transforming new love relationships with each other.

God's Mission Vision is this:

•*And all peoples (groups) on earth will be blessed through you* (Genesis 12:3).

•*Therefore, go and make disciples of all nations* (Matthew 28:19).

•*After this I looked and saw a multitude which no man could number drawn from every nation, tribe, people and language* (Revelation 7:9).

•*They will call him Immanuel—which means, God with us* (Matthew 1:23).

•*For where two or three come together in my name, there am I with them* (Matthew 18:20).

A new command I give you: Love one another. As I have loved you, so you must love one another. By this, everyone will know that you are my disciples, if you love one another (John 13:34-35).

Chapter Seven: God's Mission Vision Is <u>Accountable</u>

During the eighties, God moved Mission India from employing general mass distribution of Scripture to using three training programs: church planting, adult literacy and children's Bible clubs. All are methods of Scripture distribution, but they are measurable, and they emphasize accountability. These three methods of Scripture distribution were begun in 1984, and by the year 2000, they had largely replaced the general distribution of Bible courses. Mission India is now achieving greater results that are measurable and accountable than it achieved from utilizing general distribution.

ICT: The Institute of Community Transformation

In 1984, Mission India developed a church planting training program, in addition to the wide Scripture distribution in which it was involved. Scripture distribution is seed sowing, but by itself does not constitute the complete ministry to which we are called in the Great Commission. A farmer does more than plant seed. He grows, harvests, and measures the crop. We are called to do the same.

Mission India started a vocational training program in which the students actually planted churches while they were being trained. The training consisted of one month in the classroom, followed by three months of application in the field practicing what they had been taught. This format was repeated three times throughout the year, with the students reporting stories of successes and failures that they encountered in their fieldwork.

A very gifted Indian director, J. Chirangeevi, started the program at two locations, one in the north and another in the south. He soon found out that it did not work well, since the students were removed from their local fields of work and received their instruction and training in two big cities.

When they finished their instruction, they had a tendency to look at their diplomas with a false sense of pride and a superior attitude. They had been to the big city, and some returned to their local fields with a crippling pride.

Mission India decided to make two changes: to reduce the class size to 12, and to hold the classes in local churches, hiring and training the pastors to be the teachers. In other words, we shifted the training to the area where the work was to be carried out. This worked so well that one of the first students, who was also a pastor with a well-established church, trained five of his elders to form five witnessing prayer cells each, in five adjoining villages. Thus, in the year of his training, he was successful in planting 25 prayer cells, which became the basis of five new churches. Another pastor was trained around 1990. When Mission India interviewed him in about 2001, the people he had trained had only planted 3,000 new churches, not the 7,000 he had set as his goal!

Mission India soon had a backlog of applicants, which grew to an average of three to four thousand church planting students per year. Moving the schools to the local churches not only alleviated the need for a campus (the church was expected to provide this at their expense), but it also kept the students near their work. It also assured the students of the prayer support of the local church. In addition, working out of the local church building made them realize that this was their program, an Indian program, and not some foreign or Western program imposed on them. It helped them to realize the benefits of self-finance. The churches planted would be an extension of the local, Indian church and not some Western mission. The mix of classroom work with actual fieldwork proved to be most effective. Each student was required to call on a specific number of homes, and that aspect of the training proved to be the most important of all the learning experiences.

The India staff quickly caught on to the three parts of learning, namely: *learn it, do it, account for it*. Once these three aspects of learning were drilled into the staff, they began to understand the lack of results that they had seen from attendance at many conferences where the learning was not implemented, and the participants were not held accountable for what they did with what had been taught to them.

Primary factors in starting a church are prayer, physical healing, and spiritual healing (casting out of demons). In David Stravers' 1987 field report, he mentions that in one new Indian church, he observed that all of the new converts except one had had some experience with liberation from the demonic. The one who did not report liberation from demonic presence had had a dramatic healing experience.

Daniel is a good example of this. He enrolled in the church-planter training program because he realized the need for such training. He had worked to spread the gospel in his little village without results for ten years! When asked what strategy he employed, he said that he had preached in public areas, telling people about heaven and hell and asking them where they would spend eternity. In the church-planter training, he was taught that such an approach was fruitless, a fact that he knew well from personal experience.

Daniel was taught to begin in prayer, prayer that God would bind the demonic activity in the village, a village that was under the influence of a Hindu priestess who claimed the gift of healing. In addition to daily prayer, he and his team prayer-walked around the village many times. They recognized four powerful demons whom the priestess worshipped. They were in the four idols of the village. The priestess herself was demon-possessed. Her power of healing came from these demons.

When the priestess failed to heal her husband, she came to Daniel appealing to him and his team to pray over her sick husband and ask

Jesus to heal him. Daniel eagerly did this. Christ showed his power, and her husband was cured. Daniel then asked the priestess if she would like to be set free from the demons, and she said "yes." Daniel and his team prayed for her, and the demons fled. She became a follower of Jesus, and the villagers soon followed.

This story is unique in the sense that Daniel had worked for ten years to spread the gospel without success. It is not unique in the sense that within a year of the husband's being healed, about 50 new believers were worshipping Jesus. They met the Lord who was stronger than any demon that had troubled them. Prayer, healing, and freedom from the demonic were the key factors in prompting the villagers to search for Christ. Bible study in small cell groups came next. The Indians are often characterized as being the most religious people on earth. They quickly see the power of Christ, and they are greatly motivated to know more about him.

John Selvaraj was also an early student in the School of Evangelism (SOE), as it was first called. John enrolled in the SOE and learned about the power of prayer. He had prayed over a daughter of his neighbor who was demon possessed. Through the spiritual healing of this girl, he was able to start a Bible study in her home; that quickly became a prayer cell which matured into his large church, named *Peace Blessing*. It now numbers more than one thousand members. Each year, the number of new believers for the year's goal is painted on the front of the church. His young people are so committed that they meet for prayer each morning at 5:30.

John had fainted from heat exhaustion while visiting a nearby village. He had been carried into the village by two young men. The village was the home of two Hindu priests. One of these priests had nearly died from diabetic-induced gangrene in his legs. His flesh was rotting, and the sores in his lower legs and feet smelled so bad that his entire family stayed out of the house, waiting for him to die. During these moments, as death drew near, the priest called on his gods and they appeared to him in ugly forms, scaring him and doing nothing to heal him. He called on the name of Jesus, and Jesus appeared, asking him what he wanted. He replied that he wanted to be healed, and he said that if Jesus would heal him, he would serve only him for the rest of his life.

Jesus did it. The priest was healed instantly, and got up, walked out of his house, and showed his legs and feet to his family. His family nearly passed out from the shock of what they saw. Before he went to his family, but after the healing took place, he asked Jesus, "Who are you?" Jesus replied that in three days he would send a man to him to answer that question. Jesus said that this man would come to the village to teach him. A picture of John Selvaraj appeared in the healed priest's mind. He had no idea who John was.

The two young men who had carried John into the village called this man whom Jesus had healed, thinking he was still a Hindu priest. The healed priest quickly came to John, and looking at him, saw that he was the person he had seen in his vision three days earlier! John led the priest to Christ, and he became a member of one of John's church-planting classes. He took the name of "Jesus' Feet" and he, along with the other priest, who took the name of Cornelius, planted a church in the village. A movement of church planting started with a miracle of casting out a demon from a little girl. John has trained hundreds of church planters, who in turn have planted hundreds of daughter churches. His Children's Bible School attendance is measured in the tens of thousands of boys and girls.

Missions and churches applying for the church-planter training are carefully screened by the Mission India staff. The first question asked is, "How many churches do you plan on planting?" Any candidates who have a goal of less than one hundred are not admitted.

After experimenting in 1984 and 1985, the church-planting training took off; by 1989, it had grown to 260 students. In addition to the church planting, general Scripture distribution of gospel portions, New Testaments, *Great Bible Truths*, and Bible courses continued. During 1988, a record 12 million portions of Scripture were distributed, and if one uses the government statistic that every piece of literature is read by 10 people, this means that nearly 120 million people were exposed to the Bible during that time!

Adult Literacy

In 2000, "Chirie" (Dr. J. Chiranjeevie) and his wife, Kamala, became the India leaders of the ministry and were instrumental in making each of the ministries truly Indian. Chirie and Kamala have been the heart of Mission India in India. Chirie was the first director of the School of Evangelism (SOE) and the originator of its largest program, the Children's Bible Clubs. Kamala worked with Dr. Joyce Scott in the development and writing of the Adult Literacy ministry, and since 2000, she has been the Ministry Director of all three ministries and has developed the adult literacy program in thirty-five different languages. The prototype included printing Scripture verses for memorization on every page of the primers, much like the *McGuffey Readers* that played such an important role in the early education of Americans. God had his hand in this ministry, and it quickly flourished. Kamala was very careful to solicit the government's input in the development of the various primers, and she has developed the program with government approval.

Stories began to pour in of incredible transformation, not just of people but also of families and entire villages. Kamala developed an Indian method of enrolling students in the Adult Literacy programs. She trained the staff to put on motivational skits in the village that illustrated two types of blindness, one that is incurable, and the other, which can be cured. She did this by getting the staff to act out a scenario with two people waiting for the bus; one was blind, the other was illiterate. The blind person asked the illiterate person to watch for a specific number bus, but this was impossible for the illiterate person, since she was also blind in the sense that she could not read. All people who cannot read are blind but joining a literacy class can cure that kind of blindness.

One day a mother of four watched the skit as the Mission India staff performed it in her village. She had never considered herself blind because she could not read. This was a new idea. She thought that this might be the reason her husband beat her so often, and why her children were disobedient, and why she felt so worthless and depressed. She told her husband about the skit and asked his permission to join the literacy class that met five nights a week for a year. In this class, she would learn how to count so that she would no longer be cheated in the market place. That would make her husband proud of her. He agreed and said she could attend.

In the first three months of class, Selvie learned how to add and subtract, and much to her delight, this new skill enabled her to catch the produce sellers at the market when they tried to cheat her. Proudly, she showed the correct change to her husband; he began praising her, and the beatings stopped. Her husband actually seemed proud of her. New worlds opened for her as she progressed, proving that she was an exceptionally gifted person. She saw how important education was through her own experience, and she insisted that her four children attend school. She helped them with their homework at night.

Selvie did so much more. She learned how to make money sewing, and, with the help of the literacy teacher, she obtained a sewing machine from the government. The literacy teacher taught her how to sew with it. Imagine her husband's pride in her, when she was no longer cheated in the market and was actually making additional money by sewing for others.

Selvie faithfully memorized the various Bible passages at the bottom of each page of her primer, and she accepted Jesus as her new Lord and Savior. Her husband was so impressed with the transformation in her life that he, too, became a believer. Selvie started a "community prayer cell" in her home, and her classmates asked her to show them how to form additional prayer cells. She helped the other students in her class, and by the end of the year, she had helped to start four more village prayer cells.

During these months as she met nightly with her class, Scripture was being distributed in a very effective way. The class members memorized the verse at the bottom of the page and would recite it the following day, with great pride!

As the class progressed, the teacher kept insisting that the students save money, not spend all their money. The thirty women in the class decided to form a credit union and pool their funds. With the help of the Mission India teacher, they learned how to save and set up a fund to help each other start small businesses. Each woman received a savings book, and in it the amount each saved was carefully recorded. The women could borrow from the fund to start a business, such as making pickles, candles, or even mosquito repellant. That little slum area near Madras was soon transformed, as the average income of the students increased in that first year of learning, and they were able to make improvements to their living conditions!

This Adult Literacy Project grew rapidly, and in a few years, Kamala started what was called the Village Rehabilitation Project. This project concentrated on bringing literacy to clusters of villages and areas of at least 1,500 people during a four-year period. This project had a much broader context than merely teaching the participants to read. Participants in this project were taught about political awareness, personal hygiene, and community sanitation. They learned how to establish simple saving plans and community cooperative programs to lift the village's economic level. Most importantly, during this time, many of the participants accepted Jesus as their Lord and Savior.

At the end of the four-year period, one of the women was elected director or chief of the whole area. She brought in electricity, paved the roads and re-organized the school, so that not fifty, but five hundred, boys and girls were attending. Lush gardens were planted around many of the homes, providing fresh vegetables for the families. Diets improved. Participants built outhouses, and community sanitation was dramatically improved. Government programs, such as the distribution of sewing machine grants became available. Most important of all, the community built a community building which served as a worship center where a very active group of believers met regularly on Sundays.

In the Adult Literacy ministry, 88% of all who enroll graduate, and these graduates whose lives have been transformed are also transforming their communities. For every four classes of 30 students, about three new churches are planted. After thirty years, 200,000 people have graduated from the program, and villages in all sections of India have been transformed! The literacy program is now available in over thirty of the major languages of India.

The role of a widow in India is the least of the least. A widow is, in the minds of the villager, a spoiled commodity. There is no government help available to her. After the death of her husband, even her remaining family members do not accept her. She is a total reject, placed on the scrap heap of humanity. One such widow lived on the outskirts of her village, in a flimsy canvass tent that had nothing but a dirt floor. She enrolled in a literacy class and learned to read and write. Then she became a member of the new credit union that the members of the class formed, and she was able to borrow enough money to buy a goat. She discovered that she had a talent for raising goats, and within a short time, she had earned enough money to purchase a whole herd of goats. She used the money she earned from raising goats to purchase a more permanent shelter, a house with a poured concrete floor. Her status in the village rose and her face was transformed as she wore a constant smile. When this woman gave her testimony, she concluded it by saying that her love for Jesus had totally transformed her life.

I had taken a tour group to observe a literacy class. It was late at night. Since there is very little twilight in India, it is dark, very dark, out in the Indian countryside when the sun sets. We waited and waited that night for the class to show up. No one came. I started to round up the group to get them on the bus. The literacy class teacher pleaded with me, "Wait just a few more moments...Please! Don't leave!" Suddenly out of the darkness, a parade of beautiful women came, dressed in their best saris, with fragrant white flowers in their beautiful, black hair. The teacher was very excited. "See," she said, "These women have been working in the field all day. They wanted to shower and clean up before appearing here before your group, because, for the first time in their lives, they feel valuable. All their lives, they have been taught that they are sub-human, of less value than an animal. But, now they can read and write. Their self-image has been transformed, and they feel like queens now. Look at their clean saris. Look at them! Look at the flowers in their hair." Indeed, they were a beautiful sight. They were transformed from the inside out by the love of Christ and their new identity in him."

We both all stood, with tears of joy running down our cheeks, praising God for his loving work in their lives. These literacy classes are a most rewarding way to distribute the Bible!

The Children's Bible Clubs and After School Clubs

The year 1984 was a landmark one, for it was in that year that Mission India adopted its three primary ministries. As of this writing, the Children's Bible clubs, begun by Dr. Chirie with a hand-full of volunteers in less than ten villages, has grown to 6,000,000 boys and girls in annual attendance, and it is operating in all areas of India. However, Mission India could double the 80,000 volunteer teachers and helpers who work in CBC each summer! We must turn way that many each year due to lack of funds.

The Children's Bible Club is a two-week, ten-lesson program provided for five different grade levels. Each year, a new curriculum is developed. Each year, new songs for each language are either selected or composed. It is through these songs, accompanied by dancing, that the children bring the gospel home with their dancing and singing. Parents are thrilled that their children are happy and excited and wonder what has changed their children.

The attitude of the parents is illustrated by the story of a mother of five children who severely rebuked one of the American visitors, because only one of her children had been allowed to attend the club. She was a Hindu, a mother of five! The leader of the group explained that only one child per family could attend, because of the limited funds available. With a big smile on his face, he turned to the visitor and said quietly in English, which the mother did not understand, "Wait about six months, and this mother will be a Christian. That's all the time it takes for parents to see the dramatic transformation this program brings in their children."

Prasad was a 13-year-old boy when his mother sold him. His father was an alcoholic, as many poor Indian fathers are. He spent his wages on liquor, was drunk most of the time, and had little money left for his family. His youngest son had been badly burned when he fell into a fire. His wife had no money to purchase medicine, since the father spent it all on alcohol. This mother felt that she had no choice but to sell Prasad, the older brother, to the local landlord in order to obtain money for the desperately needed medicine.

Prasad became a shepherd. The landlord beat Prasad and told him to sleep in the cattle shed. He suffered daily beatings by his master. One day he observed a group of boys and girls singing and dancing under a tree, and he walked up to them to watch them more closely. The next day the children were back under the tree again; this time Prasad got close enough that the children noticed him and invited him to join them, which he gladly did. He heard about Jesus, but he didn't understand. While Prasad was learning the songs and listening to the Bible stories, his sheep wandered away, and he had to round them up, making him late arriving at the landlord's home and subject to another beating.

The next day the same thing happened, and the landlord, in frustration, dragged Prasad back to his mother and demanded his money back. She had spent, it and had none left, so the landlord reluctantly took Prasad back home. In spite of the threat of another beating, Prasad felt an irresistible urge to attend the CBC program the next day. He shared his story with the leader of the group, telling him about his drunken father, the lack of money in his family, and his sale to the mean landlord. The leader of the group went to the elders of the Indian church sponsoring the CBC and asked them to provide funds to buy Prasad back. They quickly raised the funds, and the next day, they went to the landlord with their money, and he agreed to sell Prasad to them. By this time, Prasad had decided to follow Jesus and had been praying that Jesus would set him free and heal his little brother. Not only did those two things happen, but his mother and eventually his father, also became followers of Jesus, and Prasad grew up to be a Children's Bible Club leader.

In another CBC program, three teenage boys stood behind the group of 200 younger children seated in front of them during the program they were putting on for their visitors. Their eyes sparkled with mischief, and the leader of the group told us their story. He said that they had been marble players, or, in other words, gamblers. They had been the terror of the town, skipping school to gamble and regularly beating up their brothers and sisters and causing all kinds of problems in their families. Interestingly, the three came from a Muslim family, a Hindu family and a Christian family. All three accepted Jesus and had been transformed into model children, loving their siblings, excelling in school, and demonstrating respect for their parents. Previously, they had driven their parents to despair with their bad behavior; now their parents were mystified by their transformation. With their curiosity aroused, all three sets of parents became involved in a Bible study led by the leader of the CBC.

By the turn of the century, CBC had grown to several million children each year. One eighteen-year-old young man, who had been appointed by a local terrorist group to be a spy in a CBC, joined a CBC to find out what was going on. He became so impressed that he gave his life to Christ, and over the next decade, he led 38,000 boys and girls in his own CBC movement.

Many of the CBC groups did not want to stop meeting and continued meeting after school. This grew into a year-round, after-school movement that included providing tutoring and limited sports activities. Public education in India, especially in rural and slum areas, is hopeless. Teachers often fail to show up. Therefore, the Christian teachers were moved to continue to meet with the students with whom they had bonded during the two-week Bible School event. This movement grew, and Mission India staff began to sponsor after-school clubs, developing a curriculum for them. This movement has grown into a complete ministry program, with thousands of year-round, after-school clubs meeting all over India.

The first result of the introduction of these three programs is transformation. The transformation of younger children brings about the transformation of family members. Since India is a prayer culture, the family members begin praying together. The transformation in the family members is noticed by neighbors, and a local prayer cell is formed which grows and often combines with neighboring prayer cells to form a church. Through the church, on-going Bible study and weekly worship is offered, and it is linked to the church planter's mother church. Without the community-wide prayer cell, the gospel will not spread, for it is in this local expression of the love of Christ that the community sees the transformation and love of Christ lived out.

Mission India's focus on these three ministries, rather than on the massive, generalized Bible distribution campaigns, was led by our first India director, Dr. Donald Chapman. He had spent many years analyzing defense contracts, attempting to eliminate waste. God used him to refine MI's focus in India to these three ministries, and, under his direction, the three ministries eventually spread to and exploded in every state in India. Early on, Don analyzed the cost required to produce a new believer and compared the results of the three ministries with that of general distribution and found that concentrating on the three ministries was much more cost-efficient.

Chapter Eight: God's Mission Is <u>Dependency</u>

There is a sign over heaven's door that says, ***CHILDREN ONLY!*** *And (Jesus) said, unless you change and become as little children, you cannot enter the kingdom of heaven* (Matthew 18:3). Children need protection, provision and the knowledge that they are precious to their parents. The good form of dependency is realizing all three—I am protected, provided for, and precious to God. Sin is the absence of this child-like dependency on God.

We had been at it all day, discussing and condemning dependency in missions. We were five Americans and one Indian, and we were discussing the ways we cripple converts with cash, thus making them dependent on our help and financing. The Indian was silent all day, as we discussed the principle that we should never cripple our converts with cash. When he finally spoke, he pointed out that in Indian families, dependency is a highly prized virtue. Independent children who go against the wishes of their parents bring great disgrace upon the family name.

Dependency is a virtue. In its best form, dependency is an exchange of lives. Jesus will give me his righteousness; that is much better than my own! Dependency is the necessary platform for seeing God's Mission Vision. Isaiah 55: 8 says, *For my thoughts are not your thoughts, and my ways are not your ways.* We get frustrated when we think that God does not answer our prayers. We put ourselves in God's place when we ask him to bless our plans, but he already has **his** plans for us. We worship the work of our hands (Isaiah 2:8), rather than worshipping God. We burn ourselves out, working in our own strength, instead of depending on God's divine power.

Dependency on God is a form of prayer (I Thessalonians 5:17). How can we pray continually, as Paul instructed the Thessalonians? How can we pray and work at the same time, especially if prayer is talking with God? Prayer has many different forms, and one of those forms is the cultivation of a child-like dependency on God for protection, provision and the feeling that we are precious to him. We are of great value to God. We are God's workmanship (Ephesians 2:10), which he designed long before we were born. Not only did he design us, but he also designed the way he could use us. When a person lives life with this attitude, he opens himself to seeing life as God sees it. This *attitude* becomes the ceaseless prayer to which Paul calls us.

Because God made each of us his masterpiece, we can know that we are protected and will be provided for. We can also know that God made the blueprint for each of his children in a way we cannot duplicate for our children. He did this long before each of us was born. We are his workmanship, not our own. The constant realization that we belong to our faithful Savior, in life and in death, with body and soul, means that we live with the realization that God is protecting and providing for us in ways that are beyond our understanding, just as a child has no way of knowing how his parents protect and provide for his well-being. He only knows that they *do* protect and provide for their precious little one. Thus, there is security and joy, the joy of a little child. We become like the little boy who, upon hearing the door to his house open, called from his bedroom, "Is that you, Dad? Can you come up here?" His dad hurried upstairs. His son smiled as his Dad entered the room, stretched out his small hand, and said, "I just wanted to touch your hand!"

Mary Ghee was a missionary teacher in India. After she had worked in her village for a year and a half, another missionary came to her village and many miracles happened. The Indians were perplexed by these miracles, for both Mary and the new missionary talked about Jesus. They asked Mary if she served the same Jesus that the newer missionary served, since so many prayers of the newer missionary had been answered, and Jesus had not done anything while Mary had been there. Mary, too, was perplexed and wondered. Why were there so few answers to her prayers? Upon talking to the new missionary, she learned a simple way of praying that really didn't sound that powerful, but she decided to try it. This way of praying was to bring the problem to Jesus in prayer, ask what should be done, write down the idea that was given, and then do it.

One of Mary's early experiences with depending on Jesus to guide her occurred when a widow came to her with a sad tale about her son who had lied on an application for a government job. This woman was angry with the son for ruining his opportunity to obtain a good job by lying. Mary prayed with the woman and then patiently waited for an answer to her plea to receive guidance as to what the son should do. Instead of receiving a thought concerning the son, Mary received the thought that she should ask the woman if she had ever lied. When Mary asked the mother this question, she left in a huff, apparently offended, only to return a half hour later to admit, with tears, that she had lied many times in her life. She, like her son, was a liar. "Confess this to your son," Mary said. The woman did, and the huge wall that had grown between her and her son was removed. The son decided to tell the official who took his application that he had lied in it. At first, the official was very angry, but then he quieted down and said, "I need honest people, and if you are honest enough to come and admit to me that you lied, then I am certain that you would make a good employee." Thus, his repentant honesty redeemed him in the employer's eyes, and he hired him despite his initial sin.

Mary admitted that she was often critical of others, and that she had an ongoing argument with her next-door neighbor. She admitted this in private prayer, and she asked Jesus what to do about making amends with her neighbor. The strange answer she got was, "Give her an egg." Mary thought that this was an absurd answer, and although she had written the answer down, she wrinkled up the paper in disgust, threw it away, and went to school to teach for the morning.

When Mary returned to her house that noon, she found a chicken in her big chair, and when she chased it away, she discovered that it had laid an egg in the chair. Somewhat dismayed, she picked up the egg and gave it to one of the neighbor's children with the instruction that he should give it to his mother. Later, the mother came to Mary's house and asked her why Mary had given one egg to her. The neighbor further said that she had given all her food to her children that morning, and then she had asked Jesus to bring her an egg, one egg was enough! Mary told her the story of listening prayer and of writing out and doing the first thought that came into her mind. She confessed her critical attitude toward her neighbor. She asked for her neighbor's forgiveness, and the two became friends.

These stories, plus a number of others, are recorded in a short, self-published book called *God Guides.* Dependency on God means that we are open to even the strange-seeming ideas that the Holy Spirit plants in our minds. Whenever we have conflict with others, we should seek the leading of the Holy Spirit and write down the thoughts he puts in our minds. Before we reject them as being foolish, we should remember that his ways are not our ways.

The methods used to fund Mission India were based not so much on the use of man's common sense as they were on finding ways for its donors to experience the unique provision of a limitless God. Without this realization, we become idolaters. No matter how much good we want to do, if it is not directed by and done for God, we will worship the work of our own hands (Isaiah 2:8). Our task is to give ourselves to him and wait on him to show us the way, regardless of how lacking in common sense the way he directs may seem to us.

In Mission India, God was preparing a totally new organization directed only at India, the remaining bastion of unreached people groups in the world. We purchased a small office building, and Bibles for India began its ministry. None of us dreamed that it would someday finance 500 full-time Indian workers, housed in a one-hundred–thousand-square-foot conference center, one of South Asia's largest Christian conference and mission centers. Bibles for India grew dramatically in the next three decades and changed its name to Mission India in 1990. It now annually trains 80,000-plus teachers and supplies Bible courses that reach five million boys and girls through a variety of Indian churches.

When we depend on God for finance, we are enabled to give according to the extent of his riches. We often tragically limit our plans due to our financial situation, while God's plans have no limit, for his wealth is limitless. When we give, we are giving out of God's wealth not our own resources. God owns it all, and we have nothing to give, unless we first ask him for the gift we want to give. He will provide to us what we, in turn, want to give to his missions.

I once challenged college students to ask God to give them $20, using some totally unexpected way of doing so, if they, in turn, would give the $20 for India. Several years later, a man rushed up to me after a worship service and asked if I remembered that challenge to the students. I assured him that I did remember. He went on to say that that experience had transformed his thinking about giving, and he had been forever changed.

This same man had asked God to give him $20. Soon, a friend asked him to substitute for him for a morning by taking care of the gym where he worked. He would pay him $20 for doing so. He took care of the gym for his friend, got the $20, and spent it. The next week, as he asked God for an extra $20, he realized that God had already given it to him once, so he asked God for another $20. That week, a friend unexpectedly repaid a $20 loan. He hadn't remembered that he had even loaned his friend the money, but he was happy to get it, and he immediately spent it on something else that he really didn't need. In praying later that week, he realized that God had given him the $20 twice! He prayed, asking God for forgiveness, but he also prayed, asking God to give him the money in such a way that he could not fail to recognize it as God's provision. That week he celebrated his birthday, and among the birthday cards he received, he found one from some friends who had never given him a card or any other birthday recognition. Inside the birthday card, he found a $20 bill! He finally recognized the gift as God's provision. He said that this unique experience changed his whole attitude toward giving.

Sugar Creek Baptist church in Houston, Texas, was $400,000 in the red as they entered the fourth quarter of their fiscal year. They decided to give, ***Why Give***?, (one of Mission India's devotional books) to every family in the congregation. Without additional reminders, the church not only got out of the red, but also ended the year with an $800,000 surplus! They also had many people who had not been involved previously in serving become involved, giving their time and talents to the Lord in various church-sponsored activities. Two years later that generous spirit still prevailed.

Many believers have found that depending on the Lord to supply funds, especially for missions, has provided them with both unique stories of God's provision to share with and encourage others and all the resources they need!

Chapter Nine: God's Mission Vision Is A Calling

Who are the people who share God's Mission Vision? They are the people who know that they are called by God. When Jesus walked along the shores of Galilee, he noticed fishermen, and, without an introduction, said, "Come, follow me!" The fishermen dropped their nets, forsook their business, and followed Christ. They did not sit down to discuss the cost. They did not say that their business had been in the family for many years, so they could not afford to leave. Christ spoke with authority when he called them to be his disciples, and they recognized his position and they answered his call!

We see this, not only in the call of fishermen, but also in the call of Matthew, the tax collector. Imagine the scene; Matthew has a very prosperous, if somewhat corrupt, business. The line of people waiting to pay taxes at his little booth was very long. A stranger walked up and abruptly said, "Come! Follow me!" In spite of the thousands of denarii waiting to be collected and pocketed, Matthew heard Jesus' call and gave his life.

William Carey felt called by God to give his heart and soul to whatever task God led him to undertake. He wrote, *I am not my own, nor would I choose for myself. Let God employ me where he thinks fit, and give me patience and discretion to fill up my station to his honor and glory.* (William Carey, pg. 34.)

Some Christians treat God as if he were a cripple, waiting for them to help him out. Churches sometimes treat worship as a spiritual performance, put on for the benefit of the audience, and not as an act of worship given to Almighty God. To them everything is for the benefit of the audience, not to glorify God.

God’s Mission Vision

Every one of us would be flattered to receive a call from the Prime Minister of the world's second most populous nation asking us to serve on some commission. It would be the greatest honor of our lives. We would rise in stature among our relatives and friends because of it. Even if a state official or a local city official called us, we would be flattered. The One who has called us far exceeds even the Prime Minister of India in importance.

Look up at the stars. Count them. Let your mind wander over the infinity of space. Look at the Milky Way, that white band consisting of billions and billions of stars. This galaxy of stars is only one of millions of galaxies. What an amazing mind, and what incredible power belong to God! We cannot even count the stars, nor can we understand how they were made, or how they continue to hang in space. God is vastly superior to the greatest human being that has ever lived. Even presidents and prime ministers are dependent upon him. God who made it all knows not only your name, but also every hair on your head! This God is calling you. He is not a weak God, asking you, as a human, to come to his rescue! This is the God of all creation who created you and now comes to you and says that he wants you to serve him (Ephesians 2:10).

Scientists tell us that if we could marshal all the billions of people on earth to count the atoms in one little drop of water, and if each person could count at the rate of one atom per second, it would take the entire human race forty-thousand years to count them all! Imagine the greatness of the mind of the One who designed and called each drop of water into being.

It is this God that comes in all his majesty and all his glory and tells us that he has selected us to come into his service. No wonder the fishermen rolled up their nets when they saw Jesus! No wonder Matthew shut down his tollbooth! It was God calling.

God's Mission Vision is a Calling

Even more gripping than the creation of the stars or the creativity shown in the making of a drop of water, is the fact that the God who redeemed us is not some detached God. This is the God who has assumed our flesh and blood, who has humbled himself to become one of us. It is he who humbled himself to take the form of one whom he created; it was he who sweat drops of blood as he stared into the pit of hell in the Garden of Gethsemane. As a human, he pleaded that he would not have to go through this unspeakable agony.

If we are to enter missions, we must do it knowing that the Creator of the stars, the designer of drops of water, and the Redeemer who entered our personal hell for us, now calls us. He is not weak. He is not infirm. He does not desperately need us to help him. His church is not ready to collapse. He is the majestic Creator and Savior of the universe. He is the Ultimate Victor over all the forces of evil. When he died on Calvary's cross, he made a public spectacle of the demonic hosts. He destroyed their power and insured their ultimate defeat and destruction. To be called by him is the highest honor any human being can receive. When we understand and act on this, we will be fit to serve him.

The One who is the glorious, perfect, complete, full, and eternal Victor is the One who calls us into his victorious cause. William Carey did not come to God and offer to help him out. God came to Carey, and, with all his authority and power, laid claim on Carey's life. It was belief in this claim that kept Carey going through all the difficulties he encountered.

Paul called himself a slave of the Lord Jesus Christ (Romans 6:22). Slaves are owned, purchased, controlled, directed, and totally accountable to their owners. Paul felt God's calling so powerfully that he could only express it by saying that his was the great honor to be a slave of Jesus Christ.

God calls us to be something! So many of us are concerned with what we will do in our lives, but God is far more concerned about what we are in our inner being. God has called us to be dependent on him for everything. No other calling is higher than this or takes precedence over this. No person can excuse himself. God wants his light to be shown in the darkness and his incorruption displayed in the midst of corruption. The only way in which this can be done is through his inhabiting, or indwelling, the special people he has called to be his own. These are people who are born again, those whom the Spirit of God calls, indwells, and fills.

God calls us to be totally dependent on him and to share his vision. *But the fruit of the Spirit is love, joy, peace, patience, kindness, goodness, faithfulness, gentleness and self-control* (Galatians 5:23). The King of the universe has called us to be his branches in which his Spirit can produce this divine fruit. What is more treasured, or more valued, than persons who display love, joy, peace, patience, kindness, and goodness? A person can rise to great heights, be known around the world, and still be a miserable failure in his character. God has created us as *his masterpieces for good works* (Ephesians 2:10*).* God is worshipped most completely by completely depending on him.

Most of the speeches given by Peter and Paul were answers to questions that were asked. Why did Christians love each other so much? God does wonders through us. These wonders are the way in which we love, not only Christians but also non-Christians, and they are also the wonders of supernatural signs and miracles. So little witnessing is done by the majority of Christians, because there are so few questions asked about the wonders of our lives. Many Christians live no differently than those around them who are unbelievers. Non-believers who observe these kinds of Christians raise questions about the hypocrisy of their lives, rather than about their selfless love!

God, who calls us and lays claim to every part of our being and life is the Master of the Universe. He is calling us to holy living, and to a purity that is so dramatic that others will inquire about the difference they see in our lives from the lives around us. He is calling us to proclaim his glory and his majesty to every unreached people group in India, and to all peoples on earth!

The wonder of God is the fact that he has qualified me! I do not qualify myself. God has taken care of all the qualifications. I can be chosen for God's team because Jesus Christ came into this world, lived a perfect life, suffered and died and then rose again for me! Now he dwells in me through his Spirit. The perfect obedience I could not give, he gave for me. The punishment I could never complete, he completed for me. God qualifies us. *For we are God's masterpieces, created in Christ Jesus to do good works which God prepared in advance for us to do* (Ephesians 2:10).

A president or prime minister has not called us— we have been called by One infinitely greater, the Master of the Universe. He has called us to holy living and to heralding the gospel. He is the One who personally qualified us for this glorious mission!

Paul prays that the Ephesian Christians may *know the hope to which he has called you* (Ephesians 1:18). The word hope means eager anticipation; it means looking forward with longing and desire and passion. Hope is that which makes life glorious. A person who has nothing to look forward to, no reason for living, dies. Depression is the absence of hope. When God calls us, this call fills our life with eager anticipation.

He is the Creator, the all-wise God, the Redeemer of the universe, the ultimate Victor over sin. What a thrill to be called by this great God to service! What an assurance we have that all things will work out for good to those who love God and are called by him (Romans 8:28).

When Paul wrote to Timothy from prison, he said, . . .*So do not be ashamed to testify about our Lord, or ashamed of me his prisoner* (II Timothy 1:8). Paul was filled with pride that he was divinely called and commissioned by the greatest Person in the universe. It was a healthy, powerful sense of pride; it had no sin in it. Paul was proud of his God. Even when he was a common prisoner, held in jail with the lowest of society, he was proud of his position as one called by God, and he asked Timothy not to be ashamed of him.

The devil will do much to discourage us. We may be thrown into prison, whipped, run out of town, and beaten for Christ, but let us never lose our sense of pride in being God's own! We serve the King of Kings, the Master of the universe. Nothing but God can ever change this position to which he has called us. What men may do to us has nothing to do with what God has made us to be.

It is important to note that when God calls us, we will have problems in our life. This calling is hated by his archenemy, Satan. The devil, and all his hosts, will do all within their limited, but formidable, power to discourage us and cause us to falter. We must expect that when we follow the call of God, life will become very difficult. Yet, amid all the problems and persecution, there is a glorious peace. *And of this gospel I was appointed a herald and an apostle and a teacher. That is why I am suffering as I am. Yet I am not ashamed, because I know whom I have believed, and am convinced that he is able to guard what I have entrusted to him for that day* (II Timothy 2:11-12). Paul approached the end of his life with a marvelous sense of confidence and peace.

What else could matter more than that he had been called to this difficult task by the King of Kings, and having been called, this great Person would guard and protect his faith to the end.

Chapter Ten: God's Mission Vision Is Waiting

God's Mission Vision has four parts. These stages or phases of developing God's Mission Vision are found in Isaiah 40:31: *Those who hope in the Lord will renew their strength. They will soar on wings like eagles; they will run and not grow weary, they will walk and not be faint.* The book of Acts records times of silence, soaring, submitting and suffering. The book of Acts is divided into these four sections, and they underlie the development of God's Mission Vision. A study of this intriguing book will keep us from having unrealistic expectations. The Book of Acts brings a victorious message, but victory does not mean that God lifts us *out of trouble*; it does promise that he will carry his children *through trouble*. These four words describe the four experiences encountered while developing God's Mission Vision. The disciples waited in silence in Jerusalem, soared in Judea, submitted by running to Samaria, and suffered while walking to the ends of the earth.

In Acts 1:4, Jesus commands the disciples to return to Jerusalem and ***wait*** for the promised outpouring of the Holy Spirit. It was a surprising command. As they watched the Lord ascend into glory, they became excited about telling others what they had witnessed. To go back to Jerusalem and keep silent was contrary to their natural inclinations. Only the first chapter of Acts is devoted to waiting for the Lord.

Waiting periods occur in the life of every Christian and of every church. Waiting periods are strengthening periods. While they are often uncomfortable periods of life, they are necessary ones, for it is in these periods that the Holy Spirit empowers us for mission. What can we learn about these times of silence and stillness, these frustrating times of waiting that are so critical to mission, but so hard to endure? It is in these times of waiting and silence that God's Spirit will change *our* mission vision to *his*. Waiting for God to act is the hardest of all the periods.

Few people love to wait. Waiting is humiliating. When we wait for someone, we are saying that the other person's time is more important than ours. Important people do not wait for others; others wait for them. If we had to wait to see the President, we probably would be willing to endure the hours needed to take our place in line; to wait for someone else who is our equal is humbling. We must know who we are, compared to God, if we are to be used by God and embrace *his* Mission Vision. Waiting demonstrates that we understand that God is greater than we are. We wait for his strength to operate through us. We are not to treat God as if he needs us; rather, we must recognize our great need of him.

A second reason why waiting is difficult is that it seems to us to be a waste of time. What good is waiting? Why go through a period of inactivity when there is so much to be done? Did such thoughts go through Paul's mind as he sat in prison when he could have been on the mission field? Did Joseph, waiting for years in prison, ever wonder about the waste of time as he was kept from doing that which he wanted to do? Have you ever wondered in times of illness why God did not heal you immediately, so that you could get about the work that you wanted to do? Why is God so silent during those waiting periods? One of the most important lessons we must learn in waiting is that God is not as interested in what we do in our own strength as he is in what he will do through us. Waiting for God trains us to be dependent on him.

A Mission India church planting student decided to do his fieldwork among a very remote tribe. It took five days of very difficult walking conditions to get to the people, and when he arrived, he met with the elders of the tribe and told them that he had come to bring them news of the true God. The elders became very excited and asked him his name and his family. It was then that a most amazing story unfolded. Thirty years prior to his coming, the chief of the tribe had disappeared. A legend grew that he had gone away to find news about the true God and would someday send his son to tell the tribe what he had discovered. The people of this tribe had reserved seven acres of land for the son's use when he returned. The elders discovered that this student's father had indeed been their chief. What great joy they had as the son told them the news about the true God for which they had been waiting all these years!

There are thousands of tribes and people groups still waiting throughout India, waiting with the hope that there is good news, news that a God exists who cares, loves, and has the power to free them from demonic darkness. In 1 Corinthians 1:7, Paul refers to the fact that all Christians are waiting with eagerness for the final revealing of our precious Savior, Jesus Christ. All of creation, all of God's creatures, all of the nations, and all of the Christians are waiting for God.

In Acts 1:4, Christ tells his disciples not to leave Jerusalem but to wait *for the gift my Father promised.* In this command, Jesus is telling the disciples that they are not in control of their lives; God the Father is the one who is their Lord. The great struggle of the Christian life is holding the belief that we are in control. We must surrender that thought in order for God to carry out his work through us. We must surrender to the fact that God is the Lord of all, and the ruler of our lives; he is the Father, and it is to him that we must give our allegiance. His gift to us of the Holy Spirit is the source of our power.

The disciples wanted to know when all of this would happen. Jesus replied, *It is not for you to know the times or dates the Father has set by his own authority* (Acts 1:7). By placing us in waiting periods, God teaches us that not only is he the Lord, but he is also the one who sets the times. We find this to be the most difficult lesson of life. We want to run ahead of God, showing him how much he needs us. When he does not bless our plans and refuses to work according to our timetables, we often become depressed, thinking that the ministry will fail, because it is not meeting our expectations. God needs constantly to remind us that he is the one who sets the times and seasons; our task is to wait and be ready to work as God opens the doors. Only then will we be set free from doing the good we want to do, instead of waiting for God to show us the good he wants us to do.

But you will receive power when the Holy Spirit comes upon you (Acts 1:8). A third important part of waiting for God is that it teaches us that it is *his* power, not *our* power, that is the power source of our ministry. God has delightful and unexpected ways in which he demonstrates his power. The church looks so weak by human standards, and it is often filled with corruption, inaction, and quarreling. It is obvious that the world will not be won through the human power of the church. The goal God seeks to accomplish is to teach us that our human power amounts to nothing at all. It is his power, and his alone, that makes the difference. Paul knew this well: *To keep me from becoming conceited because of these surpassingly great revelations, there was given me a thorn in my flesh* (2 Corinthians 12:7). Paul glories in this infirmity; he rejoices in it, because it is a constant reminder of the fact that his strength comes from God.

The final reason for waiting is given in Acts 1:8, God has a plan that he wants us to follow. We are not to make up our own plan. The plan is to go to Jerusalem, Judea, Samaria, and the uttermost parts of the earth. This plan is not chronological; we are to carry out all parts of it simultaneously.

When troubles come into our lives, we are to count it *pure joy*. This concept of pure joy is very often misunderstood. To most people, "joy" is confused with "happiness," an emotion that is dependent upon our circumstances. Therefore, the feeling is not permanent, and it is often fleeting, because our circumstances change constantly. Pure joy has only one source, and it does not depend on the circumstances of our lives. Pure joy is God-given. It deepens the closer we become to our Lord and Savior, Jesus Christ, seeking him constantly, and depending on, and surrendering to him more and more fully.

In waiting periods, we come face-to-face with God. The prophet, Habakkuk, displayed his right understanding of this concept of joy when he said, *Though the fig tree does not bud and there are no grapes on the vines, though the olive crop fails and the fields produce no food, though there are no sheep in the pen and no cattle in the stalls, yet I will rejoice in the Lord, I will be joyful in God my Savior* (Habakkuk 3:17).

When we enter the state where God is the sole and unmixed source of our joy, our strength, and our peace, we have entered the state of pure joy, pure strength and pure power. When we reach this state, we are equipped to see the mission to which God has called us. These waiting periods occur frequently in life, as God sees the way in which our joy and strength becomes "polluted" and is being drawn from things other than himself. Thus, he needs to cleanse us; as God works in our lives, causing us to wait and be silent before him, he is carefully working so that nothing in our lives can detract from him being the sole source of our joy, strength, and peace. All Christians experience major waiting periods in their lives. God also calls Christians to almost daily waiting periods, as he continues to polish us and remind us that he wants our total dependence and trust. God desires to have our mission vision match his; thus, he needs to stop us at times and re-adjust our vision.

Right now, you may be at a point of stagnation; your work is not expanding and may even be slowing down. You may be crying to the Lord, and he is not answering. We must be careful not to become so insistent on having our way that we lose faith in God when he does not grant what we ask in our prayers. If things are not happening as you desire in your own life, it could well be that God has placed you in a waiting period, so that you are forced to depend on him and his Mission Vision, and not on your own mission vision.

It is important to realize that not only people are placed in waiting periods! Everything in the universe is called upon at various times to wait for God as an acknowledgement that we are his creatures, and he is the Lord God: *The creation waits in eager expectation* (Romans 8:19). This is a mysterious concept, paraphrased by Dr. Ken Taylor in these words, "all creation stands on tip toe as it waits." There is an eager anticipation of the glorious day when Christ shall return and make all things new. The entire created order waits for God. It is He who sets the timetable, not we.

Chapter Eleven: God's Mission Vision Is Soaring

Isaiah tells us, *Those who wait on the Lord will renew their strength. They will* ***soar on wings like eagles****; they will run and not grow weary, they will walk and not be faint* (Isaiah 40:31). Of the four basic experiences in the Christian life, (waiting, flying, running, and walking), most of our Christian experience is spent waiting and walking.

This was certainly true in the life of William Carey. With the formation of his mission society, and his election to be one of its first missionaries, he broke into a period of flying or soaring. His dreams, visions and expectations lifted him to great heights. As he prepared to sail for India, he wrote these words: "The ship is here; the signal made; the guns are fired; and we are going with a fair wind. Farewell, my dear brethren and sisters, farewell! May the God of Jacob be ours and yours by sea and land, for time and eternity! " Carey's period of euphoria and soaring was very short lived. Before he had even landed in India, his difficulties began; he endured a month-long wait to reach land, while being within two hundred miles of Bengal. Contrary currents prevented the ship from landing. Upon landing, Carey spent seven years of uncertainty at the beginning of his ministry, as he attempted to settle into a specific area of work. Of his entire ministry, the soaring period for Carey probably lasted no more than a few months!

We find the soaring period of the New Testament church described in Acts 2-7. Chapter 2 records the pouring out of the Holy Spirit upon the disciples; tongues of fire visibly displayed this outpouring. The power of the Holy Spirit was further demonstrated as the disciples praised God in different tongues. The chapter concludes with Peter's sermon and the account of the conversion of the first three thousand believers. The next two chapters record the arrest and imprisonment of Peter and John. Chapters 5 through 7 record the account of two attacks on the church; one was internal, brought about by the lies of Ananias and Sapphira, and the other was external, the arrest and imprisonment of the apostles. Chapter 6 gives the details of the organization of the new church, including the establishment of the position of deacons. Chapter 7 relates the story of the first martyr, Stephen, who was one of these first deacons. Soaring is not an emotion; it is obedience.

As Christians, we often think that renewal and soaring refers to how we feel. We mistakenly think that they refer to feelings of excitement and passionate emotions. God tells us that renewal is a matter of obedience, especially obedience to the Great Commission. As the church soared and roared throughout Jerusalem, the believers demonstrated a dedicated commitment for sharing the Good News of Jesus Christ. While emotions were high during this period, the true mark of soaring is not experiential, but obedience. The New Testament church was at its height in obedience to the call of the Great Commission.

There are four ingredients required to soar or fly with God, and these four ingredients are found in the two descriptions of the New Testament church which are found in Acts 2:42-47 and Acts 4:32-37. These four ingredients are tied together. What makes a church grow and soar? Why do some parts of the church seem to be able to share the gospel, while other parts of the church seem dormant? The answer can be illustrated by the four requirements that are necessary to make a seed germinate.

Let us suppose that you wish to plant a crop of rice. What is it that you need to make the rice grow? Someone tells you that the rice will not grow without sunshine; so you plant the rice in a place where there is sunshine, on a mountaintop, for instance. But, the temperature there is very cool. The seed will not germinate. You rightfully conclude that you need more than sunshine; you also need warmth and heat.

Thus, you move the rice seeds to a place where you have both sunlight and heat, but unfortunately, you have chosen the desert, and still the seeds do not germinate. Someone tells you that you need water! Therefore, you move the seeds to a place that has sunlight, heat, and water, but while the seeds do germinate, they do not continue to grow and you discover that you also need fertile soil. Only when all four things are present—sunshine, proper temperature, proper moisture, and fertile soil—will the rice seed germinate and produce a crop.

This is also true of the church of Jesus Christ. A careful study of Acts 2:42 and Acts 4:32 will reveal the four things that must exist if the church is to explode. One of Satan's most clever tactics is to get churches to concentrate on just one or two of these factors and ignore the others. We see these four things present in the New Testament church:

- Praise—There was tremendous excitement about the resurrected Jesus, and about what he was doing.
- Proclamation—Wherever the believers went, they proclaimed the Word.
- Power—God continuously demonstrated his supernatural power through the New Testament church.
- People—The church was interested in each individual's wellbeing, and they were generous in sharing their resources, helping to eliminate all need.

When these four characteristics (praise, proclamation, power, and concern for people) mark a church, the church will explode into a period of soaring. Separate these four characteristics and put one in one church and another in a different church, and the church becomes weak and ineffective. Paul expresses this in I Corinthians 13. He describes three kinds of churches. In Verse 1, he speaks about typical evangelical or fundamental churches that emphasize the preaching of the Word. These churches teach that all one needs in order to grow is Bible teaching. In

Verse 2, he speaks about the charismatic church. These Christians say that we need more praise and power in Christianity to grow. In Verse 3, he speaks about liberal or mainline churches that are primarily concerned with social justice and equality among people. These churches are not concerned about preaching and teaching, or about praise and prayer. They major in social justice.

Christianity is like a rope that is made of many strands; when the strands are unraveled, the rope loses all its strength. God's Mission Vision sees the necessity for all four strands to be woven together. When these characteristics are woven together in one church, the church will explode, just as seed will germinate when the proper combination of sunlight, temperature, moisture and fertilizer is present. Separation of the four characteristic requirements, however, will result in weakness and lifelessness in the church.

In as much as we can distinguish churches that major in preaching, those that major in praise and prayer, and those that major in social justice, we have separated the church into separate strands and kept it from soaring. As we bring Christ to India, we must plant soaring churches that embrace all the strands of Christianity and major in proclamation, praise, power, and people! These must be churches in which there is a love of the Word, a tremendous spirit of excitement about the nature of God, an experience of his supernatural power, and a concern for people and the injustices that they suffer. Each little cluster of believers planted in a village or city neighborhood must display these four characteristics.

Praise

Acts 2-4 reveals the following examples of praise in the New Testament church. The disciples praised God for all his wonderful deeds in a way that everyone in Jerusalem could understand—in their own language. This is what the church today should be like; so filled with exciting praise that it captures the attention of all, even non-Christians. Is our church so exciting that others wonder what marvelous things are happening?

Signs and wonders were present in the early church, and these were the cause of outbursts of praise and awe. These signs and wonders continue to this day, especially among people who are under bondage to the devil. God regularly displays his power in the binding of demonic powers and in the healing of the sick (Acts 2:43).

The third reason these people were praising God was because of the new fellowship they now enjoyed. They were coming together with the new love Jesus talked about in John 13:33-35. No one in the pagan world of that day had ever seen people love each other in such selfless ways, as did the new Christians. This newfound commitment to each other caused them to experience the love that God had for them in practical ways, and it increased their praise to him. Unfortunately, power conflicts, selfishness, and leaders who have attempted to gain personal benefits at the expense of others have marred large sections of the church. God is not interested in spreading that brand of Christianity throughout any country (Acts 2:47).

Miracles of healing caused praise to God to increase. One of the miracles was the healing of the lame temple beggar, a man who was well known to every resident in Jerusalem because of his prominent position at the temple gate. He was made well enough to dance in praise and thanksgiving (Acts 3:9).

This passage shows us that praise to God is uncontrollable. When told not to speak about God, Peter, the very person who a few months earlier had denied the Christ three times, said, *As for us, we cannot help speaking about what we have seen and heard* (Acts 4:20). Praise had so overcome him, so captured him that he displayed a boldness he had never before possessed.

In Acts 4:24, we read, *When they heard this, they raised their voices together in prayer to God. "Sovereign Lord," they said, "you made the heavens and the earth and the sea, and everything in them."* While the Christians were overwhelmed with what God was doing among them, they did not forget who God was. Rather, his miracles drove them to examine the nature of God. A church quickly loses its desire to praise when it loses sight of who God is.

Praise is the act of giving credit to someone. When we praise God, or praise another person, we are giving that person credit both for what they have accomplished and for what they are in their being and essence. The church has been called out of darkness, sin, and selfishness to give credit to God for his marvelous nature and for his wonderful works. If the church is to soar, it must give God all the credit and not take credit for itself.

The disciples were constantly calling people to look at God and at his power in the resurrection of Jesus Christ. They were always talking about God and doing all they could to direct the minds of everyone they met to think about God. If a church is to be marked with praise, it must give God all the credit for the wonders it experiences, calling attention to Jesus, not only among Christians, but also among all people.

When we meet someone with whom we are impressed, we are excited to share the story about meeting that person. Alas, many are the Christians who profess to follow Jesus, but are not excited about him. They have eyes only for themselves, and they are eager to take credit and call attention to themselves, failing to glorify God. Praise occurs when we genuinely enjoy God and love to glorify him and be in his presence. The new Christians loved to be with Christ. *Day after day, in the temple courts and from house to house, they never stopped teaching and proclaiming the good news that Jesus is the Messiah* (Acts 5:42).

Luke emphasizes this sharing with the words: *they never stopped teaching and proclaiming.* They did this morning, noon and night. If we are to help win India for Christ, we will only do so by having churches that are giving credit to God for all that is done, that are calling attention to God, and that are excited about him. They must be churches that enjoy God, and covet his presence. They must be churches that are so excited about God's goodness that they will naturally share him with everyone else.

Jesus tells us what he thinks about people in the middle who are only lukewarm: *So because you are lukewarm—neither hot nor cold—I am about to spit you out of my mouth* (Revelation 3:16). People who say that they are followers of Christ, but whose lives do not reveal this, are great detriments to Christianity. They neither love nor hate him, but instead are indifferent to him, treating the greatest Being in the universe as if he were some meaningless, nameless servant.

Proclamation

The next ingredient in the explosion of Christianity is proclamation. Proclamation is a fascination with and passionate concentration on the Word of God. The church in Acts *never stopped teaching and proclaiming the good news that Jesus is the Christ* (Acts 5:42). Chapters 2, 4, and 5 all end on this point of proclamation. The people devoted themselves to the study and proclamation that Jesus is the Christ.

One of the major features of these chapters is the great sermons that Peter preached to the crowds. The occasion of the sermons was the explanation of the two great acts of God, the one being speaking in tongues and the other being the healing of the temple beggar. Both events demanded an explanation, and Peter gave it. In India, the gospel still spreads in the same way. Often God will move into a village, prior to the proclamation of the Word, with amazing signs and wonders which demand an explanation. A small church may be formed in a village, and people, seeing the way in which the lives of the Christians have been transformed, ask "Why?" We have no right to witness until someone asks us for an explanation for the difference they see in our lives.

Another form of proclamation occurred when Peter defended his actions before the government authorities. *Then Peter, filled with the Holy Spirit, said to them: "Rulers and elders of the people... It is by the name of Jesus Christ of Nazareth, whom you crucified but whom God raised from the dead, that this man stands before you healed*" (Acts 4:8). Not only did the crowds ask for an explanation, but the government also asked for one. Note what Peter said; he actually accused the officials of murdering Jesus Christ! He was not afraid to speak the truth as he stood before the very men who shortly before that time had incited the mobs to cry out, *Crucify him!* The proclamation of the Word is not a dull, lifeless thing, but rather it is an act of supreme courage and is often done in the face of death threats!

The third way the Word was proclaimed was in teachings to the church. The purpose of the daily gathering was to hear the teaching of the apostles. New Christians hunger to know more about the Savior who died for them, and they have a healthy appetite for discovering more and more of the truth of God's Word.

Power

The third ingredient in soaring is the continuing experience of the divine power of God. Repeatedly in these early chapters of Acts, we see miracles of God. They started here: *Suddenly a sound like the blowing of a violent wind came from heaven and filled the whole house where they were sitting. They saw what seemed to be tongues of fire that separated and came to rest on each of them (*Acts 2:2-3). The period of soaring opens with a visible sign of the powerful presence of the Holy Spirit. He brought divine cleansing, symbolized by the tongues of fire, and divine power, symbolized in the sound of the rushing wind. The outpouring of the Holy Spirit was expressed when disciples spoke in various known languages, reciting the wonders and the miracles of God. On that day over three thousand new converts were added to the church (Acts2:41). We often lose sight of the fact that the greatest expression of the power of God is not in miracles of physical healing, but rather in the transformation of sinners. As great as the miracles of tongues might be, the greatest miracle that day was the three thousand dead sinners raised to new life in Christ.

In Acts 3, Luke moves from relating the miraculous outpouring of the Holy Spirit, the miraculous praise in tongues, and the transformation of 3,000 to the healing of one well-known lame man. Because this person was so prominent, all of Jerusalem soon knew that after his healing, he not only could walk but he could also dance! Thus, a fourth type of miracle was added to the list, the miracle of physical healing.

In Acts 3:12-23, 4:8-12, and 4:19-20, the boldness of Peter and John and their ability not only to stand up to the authorities, but also to rebuke them is another one of the great miracles of this time. One need only consider Peter's obvious weakness when walking on the water and when standing in the courtyard denying his Lord. He is completely changed and is now courageous and powerful.

A fifth type of power demonstration was in the presence of God among the assembly of believers, described here as a physical shaking of the house. *After they prayed, the place where they were meeting was shaken. And they were all filled with the Holy Spirit and spoke the word of God boldly. All the believers were one in heart and mind. No one claimed that any of his possessions was his own, but they shared everything they had* (Acts 4:31-32).

God worked the miracle of generosity in the hearts of the new Christians, so they did not look to others to finance their new church, but rather sold what they had and shared it among themselves. We may be overwhelmed with signs of physical healing and the casting out of demons, but equally important in the display of God's power is the changed hearts of believers shown by their willingness to share whatever they have with others. A soaring church is not looking to others to bear its financial burdens, but rather looks to the power of God, which has made it a giving church.

The apostles performed many miraculous signs and wonders (Acts 5:12). It appears that the revelations of God's power through that new church were too numerous to count, and the usually precise Dr. Luke has to say that the demonstrations of the power of God were so diverse that he could not record all their ways. Peter and John were miraculously released from jail by an angel (Acts 5:19). God still uses his ministering spirits to intervene for the safety of his saints, but one must be careful in understanding this concept, lest he think that God *always* does this. One needs only to read Chapter seven to see that this is not so.

As we review the displays of power in these chapters, we conclude that we should never limit God's supernatural power to two common areas, namely, that of the healing of illnesses and the casting out of demons. Rather, the power of God is displayed in a host of different ways, ranging from his powerful presence in worship to the transformed lives of converts, to the emboldening of his disciples. God demonstrates his power in the generosity of the new church as well as in his amazing protective power. A soaring church is a church that is flying in praise, proclamation, and power.

People

The final mark of soaring in the Spirit is when the orientation of the church is toward people and not toward programs and buildings. Does the church exist to build bigger buildings and put on more elaborate worship services, or does it exist to channel God's love to those who are in darkness and who are physically destitute?

All the believers were one in heart and mind (Acts 4:32). Tragically, this unity that was so precious in those early days and remains worth more than any treasure is lacking in many churches. If the church is to soar out into the harvest field it needs the unity of spirit that marked the New Testament church. Not only were the new believers united spiritually, but they were also united materially as evidenced in Acts 4:32. They shared with each other and eliminated poverty and physical need among themselves. The church today needs to demonstrate this same expression of generosity.

They devoted themselves to each other (Acts 2:42). Early Christians were committed to serving. Christianity has drifted, especially in the urban areas, from demonstrating a commitment to a body of Christians to demonstrating a religious consumerism where Christians wander from church to church seeking the *best* pastor and most enjoyable worship service. Western Christianity has become individualized, and it has lost its commitment to community. Too often we reduce worship to a spiritual entertainment program performed for the benefit of the audience, rather than elevating it to an act of devotion given by the body of Christ as a thank offering to their Savior. In 1 Corinthians 13, Paul tells us that we can have preaching, and power, and praise, but if we do not have love for each other, we do not have the church and are reduced to virtually nothing!

What happened to this soaring church? It did not last very long. As the church was flying, the devil and his hosts were shooting at it attempting to bring it down. Especially at the heights of soaring the church is subject to awesome attacks. The first attack is recorded in Chapters 4 and 5 of Acts with the arrest of the key leaders of the church. We often say that we would like to be in that New Testament church, but we forget the very difficult times they faced. A soaring church is always the prime target for the devil. The devil attempted to shoot down the soaring church by having its leaders arrested. This did not work, so he attempted to sabotage the church from within through the hypocrisy and lies of Ananias and Sapphira. God responded with awesome judgment, and great fear seized the entire church. Satan hit his mark and temporarily crippled the church.

A third attack came, again from within, in the grumbling of the widows recorded in Acts. One wonders how long it took to change from the spirit of unity described in Acts 4:32 to the spirit of grumbling and complaining found in Acts 6. Not only was there grumbling, but the grumbling took the form of racial division: *In those days when the number of the disciples was increasing, the Grecian Jews among them complained against those of the Aramaic speaking community because their widows were being overlooked in the daily distribution of food* (Acts 6:1).

The soaring period ends when the officials of Jerusalem kill the first Christian martyr, Stephen. Luke tells us that godly men buried Stephen and mourned deeply for him. There was sorrow and sadness, and the period of euphoria had disappeared. The devil brought down the soaring church from the heights of its initial expansion into the third period of the Christian life, submission to God's redirection.

Chapter Twelve: God's Mission Vision Is Submission

A realistic view of the cycles of God's Mission Vision is necessary if we are going to be faithful in mission and develop a godly mission vision. If we are filled with fantasies about what we will experience, fantasies not related to reality, we will be defeated. A soldier entering war does not imagine he will be facing easy circumstances. He knows well that the enterprise will cost him dearly in suffering, pain, discomfort, and perhaps even his life. It is this realistic view that keeps him going; he knows what is coming, and he is not overwhelmed and embittered when the battle rages.

The new church was plunged into spiritual warfare. As we saw previously, even in the moments of initial conquest and heady victory, the devil was there shooting at this soaring eagle. He pounded that new church with the arrest and imprisonment of its leaders, with hypocrisy and lying, with grumbling and complaining, and finally with the death of Stephen.

The disciples waited for God in Jerusalem, and the Spirit, poured upon them, carried them up for a short time on wings like eagles. However, beginning in Chapter 8, we find a new story unfolding, a story of suffering, pain, and hardship. Persecution dispersed and broke up the new church. Christians escaped Jerusalem. It seemed as if God had departed and left them on their own, and everything they had hoped for came apart. It is important for Christian workers to prepare for this period of retaliation by Satan, this period in which the work seems to falter and stop after a period of roaring forward. Every missionary and every Christian experiences it. If we are unfamiliar with the period of submission to God, we can grow bitter and frustrated. Acts 8-12 records a period of confusion, redirection, and intense trial. This period in Acts covers these key events:

•The destruction of the Jerusalem church through persecution;
The redirection of Philip from a ministry to thousands to a ministry to one;
•The addition to its ranks of the church's greatest enemy, Saul;
•Peter contradicts centuries of Jewish teaching about what is clean and unclean;
•The official church is convinced that it now must admit unclean people;
•James is killed, but Peter is set free.

These events must have been confusing to the New Testament church. They teach us that after the initial period of soaring, there will inevitably come a period of discouragement and heartbreak. It is necessary for us to prepare for this period, so that the disappointments of the set- backs do not cause us to give up the mission. William Carey once remarked that he did not want to be remembered as a visionary. He wanted to be remembered for his faithfulness, his refusal to be discouraged, and his willingness to be redirected.

The church's opportunity to submit occurred when God redirected it through the very painful circumstances of the dispersal of the Jerusalem church (Acts 8:4). The church in Jerusalem had begun to settle in, enjoying the good will of all in the city, and then God redirected it. Abraham was seventy-five years old when redirection came to his life, and he had to leave his wealth and his settled life in Ur of Chaldees to become a pilgrim. Redirection often happened to William Carey when he first entered India. He arrived with high hopes and dreams, but God redirected him in painful ways. This redirection of our lives is under God's powerful control and it happens according to his unique, secret plan. The devil attacks with attempts to bring obstacles to the spread of

Christianity, but these obstacles are actually within God's sovereign plan, and he uses them to spread the gospel.

God redirects our lives into areas that are unexpected and unplanned by us. This is one of the thrills of a close walk with God. God may be on the verge of making us suddenly travel a new road that may provide new vistas of his beauty. The goal of our existence is to know God and enjoy him forever. God does not want us to remain upon some mountaintop, with only one view of his splendor and his majesty. He constantly redirects us for his ultimate purpose, so that we may view new vistas of his glory and his majesty.

On that day a great persecution broke out against the church in Jerusalem. and all except the apostles were scattered throughout Judea and Samaria (Acts 8:1). This short sentence describes a multitude of problems and pain. The new church settled down and enjoyed a steady growth, and the new converts met daily to praise God and to share their material possessions with one another. It was a comfortable, exciting existence. Suddenly God redirected the church from knowing comfort and excitement to experiencing pain and trouble. In reality, the entire church was broken apart and scattered abroad. Many had to run for their lives. Imagine yourself in that position! What would you feel like? We often fantasize about this early church, dreaming about how wonderful it would be to have a church that was so active, so wonderful, and so powerful; we forget that this church was a troubled church.

As the church was redirected, Philip, one of the early evangelists, had a surprising redirection of his life. Because of the persecution, he had entered Samaria and conducted one of the first successful major, citywide evangelistic campaigns. Jews hated Samaritans. Jews would not even walk *through* the city of Samaria! Luke tells us, *there was great joy in that city* (Acts 8:8). Rather than leave Philip there, however, God's angel redirected him from a ministry to thousands of people to a ministry to one person. Philip suddenly found himself in the desert, serving one man, an African.

One of the most amazing stories in all of Scripture is the story of the conversion of the archenemy of the new church, Saul. Breathing out threats and murder against the Christians, Saul encountered a great light on the Damascus road and God claimed him for Christ's service. Not only did God redirect Paul’s life, but he also redirected the entire church, through Paul’s ministry.

Perhaps the Indian Christian, living in the background of the caste system, with all its rigorous rules about eating and association with others, can better understand the tremendous redirection of Peter's life. Taught through his entire life that Jews were not to touch that which was unclean, God redirected Peter to accept all people. The walls of caste came down, and Peter was directed to go against all that he had been taught on the subject of uncleanness. The leaders of the church who remained in Jerusalem through the persecution were also redirected. They, too, had to believe that which was contrary to centuries of teaching. At the council, they accepted Peter's amazing account of his call to go to the Gentiles.

Finally, the church experienced a great mystery: Why had God allowed the killing of Stephen, yet, others escaped? Why did God allow James, the brother of John, to be killed, yet, he delivered Peter from prison? The point of these stories is to show that the Christian life is always changing, always being redirected by God. A new church is scattered, a ministry to thousands is reduced to one, the doors held closed for centuries are opened, and one is taken, yet another is saved. We must be very, very careful as we lay plans to bring God's Word to India so that we do not become so involved in our programs and strategies that we forget that it is God who directs our lives in the most unexpected and sometimes disturbing ways. If we are prepared for change, if we are ready and willing to lay our plans aside and watch God at work, we will become much more effective soldiers in the battle. Remember, Satan's strategy is always to encourage us to hang on to our concept of mission, instead of God's, because God's strategy will often defy common sense, and be built on divine sense.

While Satan attempts to destroy the church through persecution, God always uses persecution to direct his church. It is one of the most powerful tools in bringing new life to the church. A few years ago, I had the opportunity to ask a leader of a church in the Philippines what he thought of the future of Christianity in that country. His reply was amazing: "It is very bright sir, very bright! You see, we lost ten pastors this year."

I was puzzled by his answer and replied, "I don't understand. Do you mean that ten of your pastors were martyred this year?"

"Yes," he replied.

"But, why then do you say that the future is very bright," I asked, "if you have such persecution that ten of your pastors were killed this year?"

"Oh, you don't understand," he said. "Our church is full of indifferent and lukewarm believers. That is our greatest enemy, not persecution. God is now purging us and cleansing us of luke-warmness! This persecution must be welcomed, for through it, we will be made strong!"

Throughout the centuries, God has redirected his church through persecution, pushing the church into areas in which they would not normally go. This is his missional vision—his unique way of using all circumstances. If Satan chooses persecution, God's missional vision will turn it to good. If you are undergoing persecution for your faith, remember that persecution is far more than an attack of the devil; it is a tool used by God to steer his church into new areas. While persecution originates from the devil and is an evil attempt to destroy the church, the devil and those engaged in it will stand accountable before God for the suffering they impose. God is never defeated through it.

God not only used the attacks of Satan to redirect the church, but he also used angels. *Now an angel of the Lord said to Philip* . . . (Acts 8:26). Angels are God's ministering servants, used by him for two purposes in relationship to man; they are to protect the saints, and they are to guide them. Christ appeared to Saul in a vision of burning light (Acts 9:3), and, through this appearance, his life was redirected, and his name was changed to Paul. God still chooses to redirect our lives with amazing visions.

There is a large business community in one of the southern states of India, which was seeing similar visions of light, and their lives are being changed as they come to Christ. It is also well known that through visions and dreams, hundreds of thousands of Muslims are coming to Jesus. God used a miraculous vision in the life of Peter to redirect him to new areas. Unquestionably, God still speaks to us through visions and dreams. If the direction given in a vision is clearly contrary to the commands of God's Word, then it is not a vision from God. If we desire to have the vison of good that God has, then we will be subject to redirection at times, and that may involve tremendous pain.

Chapter Thirteen: God's Vision Is Suffering

If we sincerely desire to proclaim Christ to the world, then we must be ready to pay the price. If you do not wish to be persecuted, then do not preach Christ! If you do not wish to be disturbed, then do not share the gospel! If you do not wish to have pain, then never seek to reach those who are not Christians. Many Christians naively wish that they could be renewed; that they could be like the church of Acts, but they do not know what they are wishing for. They want excitement, but excitement comes with discouragement. They want progress, but progress comes with reversals.

A woman approached me after a lecture, informing me that she was a convert from Eastern religions, and she asked me this question: "While I know that Jesus Christ is Lord and Savior, I cannot understand why I have never found the joy in following him that I had as a Buddhist. One of the great temptations of my life is to return to meditation, to be lost in that great spurt of joy. Why is it that I have not found that kind of joy in Christianity?"

My response to her was that I did not think she would ever find that kind of joy in Christianity. Christianity does not provide fleeting, momentary joy as a normal pattern of life. I told her that we can choose to look in one of two ways; we can look outward on God and others, or we can look inward. Looking inward, which she had chosen, often gives immediate joy, but it soon deteriorates into misery, for there is nothing more awful than to be locked into eternal self-fascination. That is hell. To look outward toward others and their problems gives momentary pain and suffering, but doing so matures into long-term joy.

Christianity is a strange paradox! Joy is discovered through suffering and pain. Joy is unexpected. It comes in the back door. Christianity is the religion of the outward look; it is that which calls us to sacrificial and suffering service for others. If you want to be comfortable and prosperous, quiet and content, do not follow the One who called us to deny ourselves, crucify ourselves, and follow him in a demanding life of sacrifice. If you wish to have a pleasant religion, filled with grand emotional highs and experiences, then you cannot take the Great Commission seriously, for it calls for nothing short of an all-out declaration of war on the devil; when you attempt to carry it out, you will be buffeted and hit on every side!

There are only four kinds of people in the world. The world is full of miserable people. They have no ray of light in their lives at all. Then, there are the pleasure addicts. They are miserable, but they break the misery with fleeting moments of pleasure, often gained from sex, money, or power. The third type of person is the happy person. They have been converted and have learned that obedience to Christ's commands leads to a happy, contented life. These people seem to stay on a kind of plateau. They are happy, but not joyful; content but still restless. They know that there is more to Christianity, but they have not yet found it. So they carry on in their closed Christian circles, excluding their neighbors and living in their closed little communities.

Every now and then, however, one of them gets close to the edge of the plateau, looks over into the deep swamp below, and then hurries back to the center of the safe land. The scene of darkness and despair has done its work, however, and the Christian tiptoes to the brink to look again and again. Finally, one day he gets too close to the edge and falls over. Down in the smelly swamp, he wonders what has happened to him. It is miserable, and dark, and discouraging; as he gives the love of Christ to those imprisoned in the darkness of sin, God's love flows through him and transforms another person. He places that person on his shoulders (Luke 15) and carries him to the Lord. Instantly, this Christian, who has slipped into the swamp of despair, is translated to the mountaintop of joy, never to return to the plateau of happiness!

The fulfillment of the Great Commission requires Christians to get off the plateau of happiness and slip into the swamp of the lost to find the sheep, the coins, and the son spoken of in Luke 15. As the lost are found, not only is there immense, eternal, divine joy in the Christian, but heaven itself shakes with the divine party of the angels welcoming the lost to the Savior! Mission Vision begins in silence and waiting; it explodes in a period of soaring; it is redirected in submission to God and settles in for the long term of suffering for others. It is here that one finds eternal joy. *Those who hope in the Lord shall renew their strength. They will soar on wings like eagles; they will run and not grow weary, they will walk and not be faint* (Isaiah 40:31).

Acts 13-28 contains roughly half of the material in the book of Acts. We should keep these chapters in mind, for they will quickly dash any false hopes and dreams about the ease of Christianity. A witnessing church is a buffeted church. Paul, the great apostle, was never free from persecution. We need to look at these chapters not so much from the perspective of victory, as from the perspective of suffering. What did this new church endure in these early years? Acts 13-28 contain the records of Paul's three missionary journeys and his trip to Rome, and we will examine them with a purpose to see what suffering Paul endured in each of these phases of his mission career.

The First Missionary Journey, Acts 13-14

Cyprus

As Paul set out on the first journey, he had immediate success on the island of Cyprus with the conversion of the proconsul, Sergius Paulus. As the proconsul was showing interest in the gospel, a sorcerer and false prophet named Bar-Jesus opposed them. It was the first vehement, powerful opposition Barnabas and Paul had encountered, and Paul, speaking to Bar-Jesus, said, *You are a child of the devil and an enemy of everything that is right!* (Acts 13:10). This was hardly an easy way to begin a trip to win the world to Christ, and it clearly shows us that any attempt to reach all of India with the gospel will meet with immediate and powerful opposition by every sorcerer that the devil has available. Paul had a grand victory over this sorcerer and over the devil, as will Christians who work in the authority and power that belongs to them through the cross of Christ. The point is, however, that this was not a pleasant incident, nor is any incident pleasant when we encounter the powers of darkness in any form. This is war!

Antioch

The next incident occurred in Antioch. The initial interest in Paul's speech was so great that on the second Sabbath, nearly the entire city gathered to hear the good news about Christ, but the Jews were there, filled with envy at the size of the crowd which had come to hear Paul speak. Paul and Barnabas rebuked the Jews in language similar to that used on Bar-Jesus. *Since you reject it (the good news) and do not consider yourselves worthy of eternal life, we now turn to the Gentiles* (Acts 13:46). There is a great deal of sarcasm in that statement! It is not a compliment designed to win friends and influence people, but rather it is a military statement, announcing in the strongest terms that the direction of the gospel is being turned toward the Gentiles, because of the overwhelming hardness of the hearts of the Jews!

This was a victorious moment, and the Gentiles heard these words gladly—but wait, for the story is not over. The Jews were so powerful that they stirred up crowds to persecute Paul and Barnabas. Paul and Barnabas had to run for their lives. How would you feel if this incident had happened to you? Do not romanticize it or gloss it over with the distance of history. How would you feel if you strongly rebuked some Jews, and they rebounded by gaining the support of enough people in the city to run you out of town! Would you be rejoicing as you left, or would you feel that perhaps you had failed and lost the battle?

Iconium

The third incident occurred in Iconium where the initial response to the gospel was encouraging and overwhelming. Very quickly, however, a division arose within the city in which some sided with Paul and others with the Jews. The opposition this time was made up not only of Jews but also of several Gentiles. Resistance to Christianity was gaining momentum. The Gentiles and Jews, along with the city leaders (Acts 14:5), hatched a plot to stone Paul and Barnabas, but they found out about it and fled before the instigators could carry it out.

Lystra

And so, the two apostles ran to Lystra. Here they healed a lame man, and the response was exactly the opposite of what they desired! The crowds came out and worshipped them as Greek gods who had come down to visit the city. Paul attempted to stop them and tried to get in a few words about Christ, but the Jews had followed from Iconium, and they won over the crowd. They seized Paul, dragged him outside the city, stoned him, and left him for dead!

What a trip! They were opposed by a sorcerer at their first stop, run out of the city in the next two places, and then finally stoned and left for dead! This is not joy! It is suffering, pain and discouragement. Yet, Paul was not shaken. He knew that he was in a war, and he knew that he was on the Victor's side. Dr. Luke's description of Paul's reaction to the stoning states much about how Paul handled the suffering: *They stoned Paul and dragged him outside the city, thinking that he was dead. But after the disciples had gathered around him, he got up and went back into the city*

(Acts 14:19-20). Are we ready to handle suffering as Paul did, and when stoned, simply shake off the dust, get up and go right back into the city? Isaiah said that we shall walk and not faint. As we watch Paul, we see no soaring, but we do see Paul walk steadily without fainting or giving up.

Back Home for a Rest

The fifteenth chapter of Acts is an interlude between the first and second missionary journeys; Paul returned for home service. Instead of rest, however, he encountered two difficult challenges concerning division within the church. The first sharp division occurred within the Jerusalem church regarding the practice of circumcision. Paul and Barnabas were brought into it and sent to the meeting in Jerusalem where the matter was discussed at some length. The controversy was resolved, and Paul and Barnabas returned to Antioch where they settled down for a time and taught and preached God's Word.

After a period, Paul suggested taking a second trip to visit the areas where they had brought Christianity; a sharp division over whether to take John Mark broke out. We often lament the division that marks the church today, but we need to return to realism! Division also marked the careers of the first missionaries. They, too, could not agree on everything.

The Second Missionary Journey, Acts 15:36-16:10

On the second mission journey, we note six things that Luke records as definite disappointments.

Galatia

Paul had his heart set on going into Asia, but in Acts 16:6, we are told that they were prevented from doing this by the Holy Spirit. We have no way to know what means the Spirit used to keep them from going where they had planned to go. We only know that this is a most common experience for many missionaries. William Carey experienced it frequently during the first years he spent in India, and most other missionaries will feel a burden for a place and yet never be able to go there. Frequently, people will state that for years they have had a burden for India but have been prevented from doing anything to help in the spread of the gospel. Inevitably, this is spoken with sadness and regret. Paul must have felt some frustration when the door to Asia did not open.

Philippi

Paul entered Philippi only to be followed by a slave girl who was demon-possessed and who kept on embarrassing the missionaries by shouting, *These men are servants of the Most High God, who are telling you the way to be saved* (Acts 16:17). Luke tells us that this shouting went on for many days, obviously to the great hindrance of the spread of the gospel. Finally, *Paul became so annoyed that he turned around and said to the spirit, "In the name of Jesus Christ I command you to come out of her!"* (Acts 16:18). Why did Paul wait so long? Could it be that he sensed there would be uproar in the city if he cast out this spirit? That is precisely what happened, more trouble! This time Paul not only wound up in prison, but he was also badly beaten!

Thessalonica

After his miraculous escape from prison and the conversion and baptism of the jailor, Paul moved on to Thessalonica. Perhaps here he would be free from persecution for a few months. Unfortunately, the quiet only lasted three weeks before the inevitable explosion came; a crowd rushed the house where they were staying and arrested the homeowner, Jason. During the commotion that evening, Paul and Silas, who were in hiding, slipped out of the city and went on to Berea.

Berea

Paul and Silas moved on. God used the constant persecution to keep moving his servants. How much easier it would have been to settle down in one area and work for many months or years to establish a solid and lasting church! Instead of the comfortable, happy life, however, Paul and his companions were constantly on the run, always threatened with imprisonment, beatings and even death. Berea was no different; the initial response to the gospel was wonderful, but soon the Jews came after Paul, and his friends had to whisk him away to Athens where they left him all alone.

Athens

Paul, with time on his hands, walked the streets of Athens, impressed with the religious nature of the city. He must have sensed the great possibilities that this center of learning and culture had for spreading the gospel, and he prepared the most polished, articulate and reasonable speech of his entire career. The speech was probably the most dismal failure of his career; the number who responded to it was relatively small, certainly much less than in any other city. This second trip did not turn out any better than the first! Kept from where he felt he should go, beaten and imprisoned, chased out of town at night, moved secretly by friends to Athens, having no response in the capital city of the world—there is certainly more than enough here to discourage even the most committed child of God.

Corinth

The journey concluded when Paul entered, with great fear and trepidation, the sin capital of the world, Corinth (I Corinthians 1-2). Some peace and rest was afforded in his new-found friendship with fellow tent makers, Aquila and Priscilla, with whom Paul stayed. Paul devoted his initial attention to the Jews, but this quickly soured, and the old persecution returned. *But when the Jews opposed Paul and became abusive, he shook out his clothes in protest and said to them: "Your blood be upon your own heads! I am clear of my responsibility. From now on I will go to the Gentiles*" (Acts 18:6). Realizing that Paul was not a perfect man and that he admitted to having feelings of despair, this continuing harassment by the Jews must certainly have played a significant part in bringing about his curse upon them.

So dark had become the days and so overwhelming were the suffering and opposition to the gospel that God resorted to special revelation to keep Paul going. "*One night the Lord spoke to Paul in a vision: "Do not be afraid; keep on speaking, do not be silent for I am with you and no one is going to attack and harm you, because I have many people in this city"* (Acts 18:9-10). Paul's second journey ended in suffering and disappointment.

<u>The Third Missionary Journey</u> Acts 18:23-21:16

Ephesus

Paul began his third journey on a quiet note. Perhaps it was because Paul needed rest that God allowed Paul to stay and speak in Ephesus for three months. During this time, God performed great miracles through him. *Handkerchiefs and aprons that had touched him were taken to the sick, and their illnesses were cured and the evil spirits left them* (Acts 19:12). As wonderful as the time was, it ended with the inevitable uproar that occurred when the idols and tools of witchcraft were burned in a public display, causing the silversmith's guild to blow up! *When the uproar had ended, Paul sent for the disciples and, after encouraging them, said good-by and set out for Macedonia* (Acts 20:1). How much Paul had given! He must have longed to stay on to help this new church, which he probably loved more than any other church he had established. But, the suffering continued.

Corinth

Paul returned to the troubled church of Corinth only to encounter a plot against his life that forced him to move again.

Troas

In Troas, Paul's time there was so short that he preached all night, and during the course of the sermon, a young man fell asleep and tumbled from the upper story window to the ground, killed by the fall. By this time, Paul was used to seeing virtually anything happen, so he simply went down the stairs, raised the young man to life, and went back upstairs to continue his sermon.

Ephesus and Caesarea

In Paul's final two stops, he met tremendous and painful opposition to his decision to go to Jerusalem and then on to Rome. He was warned in both places not to do this, and his loved ones pled with him not to go.

Prison and Rome

The book of Acts concludes with Paul's long and amazing trip to Rome. For two years, he was imprisoned in Caesarea until, at long last he boarded a ship for Rome, only to be shipwrecked and bitten by a poisonous viper on the island. The book of Acts closes with the rather unsatisfying note that Paul stayed in his own rented house for two years and welcomed all who came to see him.

> *Boldly and without hindrance, he preached the kingdom of God and taught about the Lord Jesus Christ* (Acts 20:31).

If there is any one lesson that stands out in the book of Acts, it is the lesson that if we are to fulfill the Great Commission, we must be prepared for intense suffering. The devil will not give up his territory without a fierce fight. The book of Acts is not filled with soaring out of a suffering world, but it is story after story of enduring suffering in the world for the sake of Christ. Paul intimates that Luke does not record *all* of the difficulties he experienced. There were even more incidents than those recorded.

God's Mission Vision is Suffering

The reason so much of the West remains un-evangelized today is that the church, busy looking for renewal, does not understand that a renewed church is a suffering church! Renewal is not a matter of self-oriented experience; it is a matter of obedience to Christ's call to holy living, heralding the gospel and participating in the suffering of Christ.

God's Mission Vision

Chapter Fourteen: God's Mission Vision Ends in Joy

Let us fix our eyes on Jesus, the author and perfecter of our faith, who...
For the joy set before him...
Endured the cross... (Hebrews 12:2)

Faith fills the gap between what God promises and what we experience. Our experiences often will not match God's promises, and our challenge is to trust God in those times when it seems that he has deserted us. One of the great demonstrations from the book of Acts is Paul's tremendous faith. Little time is spent discussing discouragement and doubt. Regardless of what he was going through, Paul trusted in God. That ability to trust God bridged the gap between current suffering and future joy.

Each time suffering comes, God gives us a new opportunity to believe in him and to give him the thing that pleases him the most, our faith. In Philippians 3:10, Paul speaks about his desire to fellowship in the sufferings of Christ. Paul does not ask for ecstasy or for tremendous spiritual experiences. All Paul wants is to be so close to Christ that he can be identified with him in his sufferings.

Paul kept a record of the ways in which he had suffered, the times, and the places. He rejoiced in the fact that he was counted worthy to suffer for Christ. Paul labored in prison when he could have been out traveling and establishing churches in many parts of the world. What might have been frustrating for him was the most fruitful part of his life, for it was during this time that he penned many of the great epistles that are so important in our Christian faith.

How could William Carey have made it through those difficult years in India if he had trusted the experiences of the moment rather than the promises of God? Buffeted on every side by closed doors, heat, exhaustion, the twelve-year illness of his wife, the profligacy of his partner, Dr. Thomas, the lack of response among the Hindus, the tragic fire in the print shop, and the criticism of his own mission at home; yet, William Carey continued on. He plodded day after day with a steady commitment that did not trust the experiences of the moment, but instead trusted the eternal promises of God, even as he was not seeing them come true. Faith, in the form of a rock-solid trust in God's promises, filled the void between what he experienced and what God promised. Faith enabled him to lift himself from the discouragement and heartache of the moment and throw himself upon God, crying that he did not understand; yet, he did believe that God was faithful and in his own time and ways would fulfill his promises. William Carey did not see the harvest for which he had labored, for it took at least two hundred years before India was ready to respond to the gospel.

Even the temptations of Christ in the wilderness were temptations to disbelieve. Satan attempted to get Christ to base his judgements on the experience of the moment rather than on the Word of God. In attempting to get Jesus to turn stones into bread, to jump off the temple, and to bow down and worship the devil, he was saying that Christ should make his own experience the basis of belief, not the Word of God. He tempted Christ to use his power by turning stones into bread and, thus, to trust his experience rather than God's Word! The same was true for casting himself off the temple.

The devil's reasoning was that promises were of little value if they were not experienced. "Base your faith," the devil says, "on the experience of God sending his angels to take care of you, rather than on God's word." When the devil tempted Christ to bow and worship him, he offered Christ a way to escape the pain and agony of hell. God the Father says that the only way to recapture the world from the clutches of the devil is through the payment for sins; the devil says that that experience is too painful. He says not to trust God's words, do it the easy way. Every difficult situation we face will be a challenge to choose to trust the experience of the moment and doubt God, or to trust God and his Word. How we love to substitute our own version of good for God's version.

William Shakespeare wrote a play that illustrates the tremendous importance of faith and joy. There were two brothers, one good and one evil. The good brother was about to marry, and the evil brother wanted to ruin the wedding. The night before the wedding, the evil brother arranged an elaborate plot to destroy the good brother's faith in his bride. He arranged to have the good brother in the garden outside his bride's bedroom. Knowing that the bride would be gone, he placed another woman in the bedroom and had a friend climb up to the balcony and embrace this imposter. The good brother was too far away to recognize his bride; all he saw was a woman, whom he assumed was his bride, embracing another man. He became furious. The following day, in the middle of the wedding ceremony, the good brother publicly humiliated his bride, charging her with unfaithfulness. As I watched this scene, I felt sad! "Why could you not wait," I asked myself, "Why could you not investigate? Why are you so quick to believe your feelings of the moment? You will never be able to take back the things you are saying to this innocent woman."

Is there a greater gift that we can give a friend than to say, when all the evidence points to guilt, "I still believe in you, and I am still committed. Something is wrong. I know your character, and I know that you could not have done this!" What a tremendous gift to have friends who will believe in us, even when the evidence of the moment may make us look guilty.

That is also true about God. The devil is the evil brother, and his entire purpose is to frame God. He wants you to look at all the evidence in life and doubt God. His constant, daily purpose is to get you to look at what you are experiencing, say that it does not match God's promises, and then become bitter and doubt God. God is watching over you, asking you if you know him well enough to trust him in circumstances in your life that you cannot understand or explain. Do you know the character of God, the greatness of God, the perfection of God? Do you know him so well that you will never trust your own experience or feelings, but you will always trust God? The faith that prefers to trust the promises of God rather than the experience or feelings of the moment is that faith which produces eternal joy.

God gives us the ability to have saving faith. We cannot believe on our own. We must be born again to receive his Spirit that enables us to believe him for salvation. Once we are born again, we are able to give or deny faith on a daily basis for the smaller things that happen. I please God, if in the midst of the discouragements and setbacks, I humble myself and do not trust the experience and my feelings of the moment, becoming bitter and judge God for what he has not done. I must not be like the good son in the play, who, without investigation, believed what he experienced and felt at the moment and wrongly judged an innocent woman.

God is innocent of all evil. He has given his only Son to die for us. If he has done so much for us, then why do we doubt that he will give us every other good thing? We doubt because our momentary experiences say that he is not giving us every other good thing. There are periods in life when it seems as if God has forgotten us. In these moments, we are called to trust his Word, and not our experiences. In these moments, we are challenged to humble ourselves and acknowledge that even though the evidence we see says that God is not faithful to his promises, we will still believe, for we are not God, and we cannot see all things. It is this kind of faith that pleases God, and at the same time, results in our eternal joy.

Abraham was called the *father of believers*. Hebrews 11:8-19 shows why he, more than any other saint in the Bible, deserves this name. He spent his entire life facing situations where the experiences of the moment never matched the promises of God. He failed to possess the land God gave him; he had no great family, save one son born supernaturally in his old age, and he was called to sacrifice that son! He only saw God's promises from afar, and if he were to have built his faith on his personal experiences, he would have had no faith at all.

By faith Abraham, when called to go to a place he would later receive as his inheritance, obeyed and went, even though he did not know where he was going (Hebrews 11:8). The first great challenge of Abraham's life came when he was seventy-five years old, and God asked him to give up all that was familiar and precious to him to go to an unknown land. The challenge was this: Would Abraham trust what he knew from his own experience, or would he trust the Word of God about a promised land that he had not yet experienced? Abraham knew that life was good; he was settled, with a large family and many possessions. He knew nothing about this Promised Land of which God spoke. He only knew that God had spoken and called him away from what he knew to an experience that he knew nothing about. God was shifting Abraham away from building his life on comfortable experiences with what was familiar to living on the promises of the Word of God and obediently entering new areas. God was moving Abraham away from substituting his concept of good for God's concept of good.

This is the same challenge that confronts all Christians today. Most of us, unlike Abraham, fail the test, preferring our comfortable, ordered lives to venture out into the unknown to follow God's call. We would rather control our lives than have God control them! We are more comfortable arranging our own finances than trusting God for his provision. We are more comfortable staying among our own family and friends than venturing into new areas where we must trust God's Word.

A missionary needs commitment to trust God's Word so that he can venture out into areas that are unknown. His entire life must be like Abraham's. The rock of his security is not to be a comfortable routine; rather it is to be God. As God clearly calls the missionary to enter unknown areas, he goes confidently, not in his comfortable experiences, but in the Word of God. He shifts his life from trusting his experience to trusting the Word. *By faith he made his home in the promised land like a stranger in a foreign country* (Hebrews 11:9). Abraham continued living as a pilgrim upon arrival in the promised land. He did not possess the land, but he lived in it as a stranger. Missionaries are called to live like strangers; they are at home neither in the land they left, nor in the land in which they minister. They have a new home, *for he was looking forward to the city with foundations, whose architect and builder is God* (Hebrews 11:10).

Most of us search for the pleasures of life rather than for the promises of God. The pleasures of this life can ruin our faith in God. The pleasures of this life can make us indifferent to the promises of God. Why should we be concerned about the promises of God for the next life when we have it so good in this life? Our earthly wealth is so enjoyable that we want nothing more; we become content with our earthly treasures that last only a few years. This indifference to the promises of God is one of the most devastating things that can happen to a Christian. One of the greatest insults given to God is to prefer the passing, trifling material treasures of this world above the eternal treasures that God offers in his promises.

One of MI's first board members founded his own relief agency and collected used medical equipment for villages in China. One time, upon delivering a container load of used medical equipment to a small village, the Christian elder asked him where he got all the equipment, and he replied that it had been used and then discarded for newer equipment.

"We must pray for you," said the concerned village elder. "How can you possibly see Jesus through all that stuff?" The pleasures of this life keep us from seeing and believing in distant and as yet unrealized promises of God. At times God allows some catastrophe into our lives. Sometimes when this happens, we move from indifference to bitterness. We become angry, because we no longer have the things that have become so precious to us.

We need faith to lead the pilgrim life, a life that is larger than the pleasures of this life, one that is not bogged down in accruing material things. We need to be able to live on the promises of God and not on the possessions of this life. Abraham was the father of believers, not only because he sacrificed the known for the unknown, preferring to stand on God's Word rather than his familiar surroundings, but also because he preferred God's promises to the pleasures of this life. This enabled him to live as a pilgrim, passing through unencumbered by a striving for the pleasures of this life.

Perhaps the greatest demonstration of faith in the life of Abraham occurred in the birth and sacrifice of Isaac, his only son. God gave Abraham the promise of a great family. His children were to be as numerous as the sands of the seashore and the stars of the heavens. In the hope of realizing that promise, Abraham left the known for the unknown and lived like a pilgrim. Twenty-five years after he came to the promised land, Abraham still possessed none of these things; then, when he was one hundred years old, Abraham and Sarah had not started their family. God visited them and asked how the family situation was.

Can you imagine Abraham's reaction? "Well, God, it is getting a little late. I'm one hundred years old! It's past time to get started, especially if I am to have as many children as the sands of the seashore!" Sarah listened and laughed in the tent! The whole situation struck her as being totally ludicrous. Here are two old people, far beyond the years of bearing children, still waiting for a family! Can you imagine the faith that Abraham displayed in light of his own childlessness, still trusting God's Word? What would you have done in his situation? How can one possibly trust a God who promises the blessing of a great family and had still not given even one child to that person as he reached the age of one hundred! Then, twenty-five years later, this God demanded the sacrifice of Abraham's one and only son. However, Abraham did not trust his experience; Abraham believed the Word of God! God had promised him a great family, and Abraham trusted that God would be faithful to that promise in his own way.

God wanted Abraham to have no doubt that it was God alone who fulfilled the promise of a family. Abraham had tried to fill the promise for God, when he took Hagar as his wife, and she bore Ishmael. God rejected that, however, and said that Ishmael was not the promised child. God wanted to birth a child through Abraham and Sarah in a supernatural way, and, therefore, waited until long after their years of childbearing had passed, so that there never would be any doubt that Isaac was supernaturally born.

God often works in our lives this way. When everything seems to be a disaster, and all God's promises seem to fall away, all he is really doing is clearing the way so that he can supernaturally fulfill his promises in our life. He wants us to look at the promises not as things that we have created, but as miraculous gifts from him. We must be brought to the very end of our resources and convinced that there is no other solution than one miraculously provided by the Almighty God.

Israel's escape from Egypt, only to face the impossibility of crossing the Red Sea, is a grand example of the fact that God loves to provide miraculous ways out of impossible situations. Israel had a three-way choice of how they wished to die. They could plunge into the sea and drown; they could fight the Egyptians and lose; or, they could flee into the desert and die of starvation and thirst! There was no human way out, as the hordes of Egyptian soldiers pounded down upon them and backed them against the Red Sea. God called on them not to trust the experience of the moment, in spite of everything their minds and emotions told them. "Trust me!" he called. As they responded with faith, God miraculously opened the Red Sea, and they passed safely through. Trust God for the supernatural; when your experience tells you that there is no longer any human way out of the situation, turn to God and say, "I will not give up, I will not despair, I will not doubt! Even though I can see no solution to this situation, I still believe you will work through it." This is adopting God's vision and opening the door to eternal joy.

Abraham was called to sacrifice that which was most precious to him, Isaac. *He who had received the promises was about to sacrifice his one and only son, even though God had said to him, "It is through Isaac that your offspring will be reckoned*" (Hebrews 11:17-18). Review what God asked Abraham to do. Abraham was to leave the known life for the unknown, and once he had arrived in the promised land, he was to live in it as a stranger, not possessing it. He was promised a family of multitudes, but when he had reached 100, he still did not have a single heir! Finally, when his heir, his only child, was born and was of age, God asked Abraham to sacrifice him as the final test of trusting God's Word rather than his own experience.

Place yourself in Abraham's situation. At the age of 75, God calls you to leave everything familiar to take up residence in a foreign land that you do not own. You have received a child supernaturally that you are now called to sacrifice. Would you not wonder about the wisdom of this God?

Yet, Abraham did as God commanded, trusting God's Word and God's provision over what he was experiencing at the moment.

Faith is saying, "I am not God! If God has spoken it, then we must believe it, regardless of our experience in this moment." When we join Eve in the garden and begin thinking that we know better than God about the forbidden fruit, then we are in for great problems, for we have taken God's place. Satan is out to frame God. He is always arranging circumstances in our lives so that we will believe the worst about God. Our challenge is to remain faithful to God, regardless of the experience of the moment, believing that if he loved us so much that he would die for us on Calvary's cross, then he certainly will not desert us in the dark moments of our lives.

All the way my Savior leads me;
What have I to ask beside?
Can I doubt His tender mercy,
Who thro' life has been my Guide?
Heav'nly peace, divinest comfort,
Here by faith in Him to dwell!
For I know, what e're befall me,
Jesus doeth all things well."

Fanny J. Crosby

God's Mission Vision is born in his goodness. It is a courageous decision built on faith that we will conquer which opens the door to joy. It involves the realization that mission work is warfare. While the ultimate outcome of the war has been determined on Calvary, there are many battles yet to fight. These can be lost if we do not know our enemy, his tactics, and our equipment, both in offensive and defensive battle.

Nowhere is the physical evidence of spiritual warfare more evident than in the land of India. In a group of 30 new believers, all but one had come to Christ after being set free from the demonic. In India, signs of darkness, bondage, and despair assail us from every side: the staggering number of people, the vast number of tribes and castes, the economic problems, and the swelling cities with their social difficulties. All of it depresses us, giving us the impression that there is no sense in waging the spiritual war here, for we shall never have victory. Mission agencies, churches and donors have deliberately turned away from India, because the battle was too difficult, and the chances of winning seemed so slim!

Paul says, *Our struggle is not against flesh and blood, but against the rulers, against the authorities, against the powers of this dark world and against the spiritual forces of evil in the heavenly realms* (Ephesians 6:12). As human beings, living in a physical world, we easily forget this important teaching that our real enemy is a spiritual one who is out to destroy God and all his creation. When others attack and persecute us, we think of them as the enemy, failing to remember that behind them is the one who is the ultimate enemy, the one with whom we are really wrestling.

When sickness strikes or disunity rips apart our mission or our church, it is not circumstances or human beings who are ultimately behind our problems; it is this archenemy of whom Paul writes in Chapter six of Ephesians. Paul tells us that we are to see the discouragements and troubles of life in terms of spiritual warfare with the devil and not as opposition from humans or as accidental circumstances. It is essential that we have a good understanding of who the enemy is.

Who is the prince and lord of darkness? Ezekiel 28:17 says about the devil, *Your heart became proud on account of your beauty, and you corrupted your wisdom because of your splendor. So I threw you to the earth; I made a spectacle of you before kings.* At one time, the devil was among the most spectacular and beautiful of God's angelic creatures. The devil's tremendous beauty and knowledge became the foundation of his pride, and he desired to take God's place. He, along with approximately one third of all the other angels, rebelled against God, and a mighty war broke out in heaven between these evil angels and the angels remaining faithful to God.

Then war broke out in heaven. Michael and his angels fought against the dragon, and the dragon and his angels fought back. But he was not strong enough, and they lost their place in heaven. The great dragon was hurled down—that ancient serpent called the devil or Satan, who leads the whole world astray. He was hurled to the earth, and his angels with him (Revelation 12:7-10). This passage not only tells us of the warfare that occurred in heaven, but it also teaches us where this battle continues to wage has been changed from heaven to earth. The devil and his demonic hosts were cast out of the holy and sinless heaven, and they are confined to this earth. It is here on the earth that this spiritual battle continues.

This battle, while having material and physical effects, is primarily a spiritual battle, waged in *the air*. In Ephesians 2:2, Paul describes the devil as, *the ruler of the kingdom of the air, the spirit who is now at work in those who are disobedient.* This unique description, *ruler of the kingdom of the air*, leads Christians to believe that there is an in-between kingdom, a kingdom between heaven and the physical world in which we live. It is this kingdom that is called *the kingdom of the air*, and both good and evil spirits inhabit it. It is within this arena that the battle of the universe is going on, with both good and evil spirits exercising influence over human beings. This spiritual world has a far greater effect upon our lives than we can imagine. The evil beings in the atmosphere are under the control of the prince of this kingdom of the air, the devil himself. The Bible distinguishes between Satan, the lord of the kingdom of the air, and the demons who are lessor-ranked entities. These are spirit beings, which occupy or attach themselves to specific persons or places. They are limited by space and time. They inhabit only one place or person.

The good angels constantly battle the demonic forces and, having removed them out of the heavens, they now are battling them for control over humanity. Christ has insured that in this warfare he will be victorious, for when he died on Calvary he made a public spectacle of the demonic hosts. He humiliated them (Colossians 2:15). Nevertheless, while the outcome of the universal war is assured, the battles continue in this present age.

As we develop Christ's Mission Vision, Paul makes us aware that we must not see circumstances, sickness, fighting with other Christians, or persecution from non-Christians as the ultimate problem. Behind all this opposition and discouragement, a tremendous spiritual battle rages, and the difficulties we encounter are to be seen in terms of wrestling *not against flesh and blood but against principalities and powers* (Ephesians 6:12).

By completing the full payment for sin, Christ opened the way for our return to him. This is the God of resurrection power. Not only did he fulfill the punishment for sin, but he also conquered the penalty of sin, death itself. He entered death and arose from death victoriously. Developing God's mission vision requires that we see the unseen demonic hosts that are attacking. We must do it celebrating the victory God gave us. He is the God who created heaven and earth, who bore the eternal punishment of hell, and who entered the grave and conquered death. He has defeated these demonic hosts on every score! *Let us celebrate!* Mission Vision sees the demonic world from two perspectives. First, how we can keep them from attacking us, and second, how we can attack offensively. How can we protect ourselves from demonic attack? Paul suggests four specific tools that we can use.

God has given us four powerful weapons that we can use in our attack against the demonic powers. First, we must put on the *helmet of salvation*, which is an attitude of victory. We must always celebrate! As we approach an area, we should have no doubt of the outcome. Christ will be victorious over it. It may not be in this specific battle. We may have to return. But the ultimate victory has been insured. *Therefore God exalted him to the highest place and gave him the name that is above every name, that at the name of Jesus every knee should bow, in heaven and on earth and under the earth, and every tongue confess that Jesus Christ is Lord, to the glory of God the Father* (Philippians 2:9-11).

Second, we must take the *sword of the Word of God* in our hand. We need more than prayer and fasting to conquer the demonic powers and scatter them. We need the Word of God. Christ himself, in his temptations, used the word of God to rebuke the devil. Both the devil and his demons respect this Word, and as we recite it, and use it in our confrontations with evil, we will experience it as a sharp, two-edged sword that both cuts down the demonic spirits and also opens the heart of man (2 Corinthians 10:3-5; Hebrews 4:12).

Third, we must spend much time in *prayer* for each other. God has given us prayer and has bound himself to respond to us. The church fails to use this instrument of prayer properly and, hence, suffers many unnecessary losses in spiritual battles. We can do all the planning, research, strategy, and training we want over a specific area, but until we bathe that local place in prayer and fasting prior to entering it, we will usually meet with dismal results.

Finally, Paul advises us to be *alert.* We can never be too careful as we engage in this work. We must always be watching, making certain that we do not open ourselves to demonic attack, and that we are using all the weaponry that God has given us in this strategic battle. Every missionary will testify to the fact that bringing the gospel involves spiritual warfare. The devil does not play fairly; he will break every rule in the book! His one goal, and that of his demonic hosts, is to defeat us in any way possible. But, defeat is not possible if we follow Christ's advice, fully equip ourselves for battle, and use the weapons he has given us. The fact is that Christ is already victorious!

Who is the Conqueror? *Know that the Lord is God. It is he who made us* (Psalm 100:3). This is a fact that we quickly forget. We need to be reminded that we did not make our body or our soul! God not only created us, he owns us. *It is he who has made us, and we are his* (Psalm 100:3). He owns us, and we are, and always will be, totally accountable to him. We must commit to him, not only because he designed us, but also because we belong to Jesus Christ with body and soul, in life and in death. God is our Father, and we are members of his family.

A*nd we are his; we are his people, the sheep of his pastures* (Psalm 100:3). In many places in the Bible, God refers to those who believe in him as his adopted sons and daughters, his family. Jesus tells us to address God as, *Our Father*. Here is the highest family commitment that we will ever make. Since God is our Father, he is the one who takes the preeminent place in our life.

Celebrating is surrendering to God. Another way of speaking of surrender is to call it praise or thanksgiving. Only those who have truly surrendered to God can fully praise him. We are to give God credit for what he has done. This means that we must put aside all selfish thoughts and ideas. We have nothing for which we can take credit. We must not be seeking credit and recognition from others. We must always be eager to have people look through us to see Jesus. To surrender to Jesus means that we get out of the way, we stop trying to get people to look at us and instead direct their vision toward God. We give him all the credit and, thus, we share in his victory.

Part Two: Mission India's Practice of God's Mission Vision

Chapter Fifteen: Start with Prayer, Not Human Plans

Haddon Robinson asked this question, years ago in a meditation from, *Our Daily Bread*: "Where was the **work** of the atonement done? Was it in the garden in the prayer of surrender, or before Pilate, or on the cross?" It is a provocative question. He rightly suggests that Jesus suffered most and worked hardest when he sweat drops of blood, praying and submitting his will to his heavenly Father. This prayer enabled him, in his human nature, to endure both the scoffing, mocking and injustice in the court of Pilate and the unspeakable pain of the cross.

When Jesus described our relationship to him as being yoked to him, he was telling us that we needed to begin on the same foot he does, namely the foot of prayer. He lived in prayer; he began the suffering of the atonement in prayer. The heavy work of the atonement could well have been the bloody sweat in the garden as he, in his human nature, wrestled to bring his human will to match the Father's will. If we start with prayer we start with Jesus, and we are in step with him. But, if we only pray, or we only work, we walk around in spiritual circles!

Most of us have never watched a team of oxen that are yoked together. It appears to happen effortlessly, as they pull the plow through the deep muck of the rice fields of southern India, walking in perfect step with each other. Looking at a team from the side, they are in such perfect harmony that one can only see one set of legs. However, the moment they get out of step, the ease is gone, and they stumble. Jesus promised us that if we begin in prayer as he did, we will be yoked with him, and we will find spiritual rest. We will avoid spiritual stumbling.

Sharing the gospel using prayer as the starting point is the primary mission principle of God's Mission Vision. In the late eighties, Ralph B., a missionary to the Muslim community in Mombasa, Kenya, had worked out a prayer that opened the Muslim's heart to consider Jesus. Ralph trained a few Kenyan Christians to call on Muslim homes to ask if they might pray a prayer of blessing on the home in the name of the Muslim prophet of prayer, Jesus. When the Muslim family agreed to this, as most did, the Christians added, "Would you also agree to pray in the name of Jesus this week, and then we will call back to see what happened?" Miracles abounded. So many turned to Jesus as their Savior that it is believed that half of Mombasa had turned to Christ.

Prayer is a common religious practice. Hindus, Buddhists, Jews, Muslims, Christians, all pray or profess to pray. One of the most common statements that can be safely made without fear of appearing to show American superiority is, "Our prayers are with you."

In 2000, Mission India adopted the B.L.E.S.S. prayer approach, which is now widely used in India while sharing Christ. B.L.E.S.S. is built on the truth that all humans are created in the image of God, they are all worthy of prayer, and the normal response to being prayed for and blessed is positive.

At the beginning of the 21st century, Mission India was reorganized. The organization was still small, but the respect given it by the Indian Christians had grown. To celebrate, a national convention was held. The organization chose the word *transformation* as the one that best described its mission. Mission India is called to transform individuals, families, villages, districts, states and the nation. The transformation theme was based on Matthew 8:1-4, the story of Jesus healing the leper as he was coming down from the mountain where he had given his famous sermon on the mount. The leper broke social customs and laws as he approached Jesus, saying, *Lord, if you are willing, you can make me clean* (Matthew 8:2).

Jesus said that he was willing, and he touched the leper. In touching him, he also broke social customs. Lepers were unclean, and no one could touch them. Jesus transformed or blessed the leper in five ways. Indians love acronyms, and the five transformations which the leper experienced are summarized with the acronym, B.L.E.S.S. Jesus touched the leper and healed his **B**ODY. Because his body was healed, he could return to work, and so his **L**ABOR was healed. Because his body was healed, and he could work again, his **E**MOTIONS were healed, and he experienced relief and joy. These three transformations produced another, external transformation. The leper could fit back into society, and his **S**OCIAL LIFE was transformed. This transformational healing occurs when someone accepts Christ and his or her body, labor, emotions and social life are transformed in various ways. All of these four *external* transformations are based on an internal transformation that is **S**PIRITUAL and comes from faith in Jesus.

This transformation is pictured as a four-sided square. Each side represents one of the external transformations; the internal transformation, trust in Jesus, is the root of the transformation, and it is placed inside the square.

Thus, the words BLESS and TRANSFORMATION became the key descriptions of what Mission India was doing. Church planting was called *The Institute of Community Transformation* or ICT. Each Indian involved in one of MI's three programs was challenged to pray for these five blessings to come on five families, using their five fingers to remind them of the letters. Little did Mission India realize the amazing, numerical potential of the B.L.E.S.S. prayer.

In the year 2016, Mission India had about 5.7 million persons enrolled in its three programs. Each person was a member of an average family of five, involving a total of some 25 million people. These people were trained to pray the BLESS prayer. Those 25 million people (5 million families of five) could each bless five more families each day, so that 125 million families could be prayed for, amounting to (at five persons per family) 625 million people. Remember, don't let common sense get in the way when you are trying to see things God's way! *Unto him who is able to do more than we can ask or imagine* (Ephesians 3:20)!

Prayer plays an important role in all religions. All religious people pray and love to be blessed by prayer. Thus, the stigma of the words, *conversion* and *evangelism*, were removed when Christians were urged to pray five blessings on five families each day, blessings which result in total transformation, external and internal, of individuals, families and villages.

Chapter Sixteen: "Don't Pluck and Plop, Flip and Flow"

In J. Waskom Picket's classic book, *Christian Mass Movements in India*, repeated references are made to the conversion story of Mr. Ditt, a member of the Chuhra tribe in northern India. His story illustrates the difference between plucking a person out of his natural group and plopping that person into a mission compound.

In 1850, a mission was established in the Punjab that employed the traditional methodology of encouraging converts to live on the mission compound in order to be indoctrinated and to protect them from the physical abuse that would be heaped upon them by family and friends. The response was minimal; few people came to know Christ. A Mr. Nattu, of the Jat caste and the son of a prosperous landowner, was converted, but he did not live up to the great expectations that the missionaries had for him. He proved to be a very weak brother; one day he brought a small, dark, lame man whose name was Mr. Ditt with him to the mission compound in Sialkot. Mr. Nattu had shared Christ with Mr. Ditt.

The missionary, after examining Mr. Ditt, found that he was well instructed in the faith, and that he was sincere in his desire to follow Christ, and so he baptized him. As was the custom at the time, the missionary, Dr. Gordon, then urged Mr. Ditt to leave his home among the Chuhra tribe and move to the mission compound, so that he could be taught the Scriptures and be protected from the usual physical persecution that was certain to fall upon him upon his return to his village.

Mr. Ditt refused the offer, preferring to return to his village; so, with the blessing of the missionaries, the door to his people group was flipped open. He trudged off to his family, which consisted of five brothers, who with their families numbered about sixty people. They would not eat or drink with him, and they heaped abuse upon him after hearing that he had become a Christian. Mr. Ditt remained faithful to his calling, however, and refused to cut himself off from Christ or from his people.

Three months later, Mr. Ditt appeared at the mission compound in Sialkot and presented his wife, his daughter, and two neighbors for baptism. He had taught them what he knew, and now they professed their faith. The missionaries examined them and found that they knew enough to follow Christ and to be baptized.

Immediately after their baptism, Mr. Ditt removed them from the mission compound and moved them back among his own people. Six months later, Mr. Ditt reappeared at the mission compound, this time with four other men who professed their faith in Christ. It was obvious by this time that God had begun a unique movement among the Chuhars. Mr. Ditt remained faithful, traveling about, buying and selling hides and witnessing to all his people about Jesus Christ. Within forty years, 300,000 Chuhars had confessed Christ as their Savior and had been baptized.

We tend to be critical of the missionaries and their early methodology. They kept new converts on the mission compound. This is the *pluck and plop* method: pluck a person out of his natural people group and plop him on the mission compound. When we do this, we destroy the natural lines for the communication of the gospel by isolating the new convert from his own people. Pickett wrote, "The effects of this separation were perhaps equally bad on the converts and in turn on the attitude of their relatives, friends, and neighbors toward Christianity. Few converts may be said to have prospered in any sense. They became too dependent—socially, economically, and religiously—upon the missionaries, and learned to think of themselves as a people apart, not only from the groups to which they had belonged but in the whole body of their fellows"

Pickett goes on to state that of fifty inquirers at that time, only seven were baptized, and of those seven, four left the faith. The individualized method of evangelism has been popularized in the West. The Western concept of discipleship removes the convert from his natural setting, makes him a member of a distant church, and there he is taught the Scriptures. The West fails to understand that discipleship is primarily the planting of new cells of the body of Christ in specific people groups. Any tendency to remove new converts from their natural surroundings sterilizes the gospel and effectively hinders its spread. The new converts often do not fit within the older church, and they become people without a people, and then they often fall away from Christ. The individualized method, by which a new convert is removed from his natural surroundings, has been one of the primary causes of slowing the spread of the gospel.

Even a casual study of the book of Acts reveals that Paul and the other early missionaries used the method practiced by Mr. Ditt. Mr. Ditt became the door to the Chuhars, which was *flipped open* through his conversion and stayed open to his own people, so that the gospel *flowed* into the group, and new clusters of believers were formed. It is easier to follow this method of evangelism in the East than it is in the West, for the Eastern person tends not to look at himself as an isolated individual, but instead as a member of a group or community. "To address him in the singular is to insult him, unless you speak as a member of his family circle or as an intimate friend" (Pickett, pg. 26). He is not a person by himself, a person apart, but rather, he sees himself only in terms of his family, village and group. To have many relatives makes him a man of great honor.

When a convert is plucked out of his normal environment, the opportunity to spread the gospel is stopped. Each person must come to Christ to be born again, but for people who are not accustomed to doing things in an individual setting, such activity is far more natural in a group setting. Pickett states, "Ask a typical villager, happy in his group associations, to take an action involving his profession of religion, without consultation with or regard for the opinion of his group, and you outrage his sense of propriety, even his ethical sense" (pg. 27). The apostle Paul always approached people within their natural context. When Lydia came to Christ, Paul used her influence to witness to her entire circle of friends and to plant a church among them. When the Philippian jailor came to faith, Paul included his entire household and saw, not only one individual who believed, but instead an entire new church that was established through this man (Acts 16). Paul saw people not as individuals torn out of their natural setting, but rather as people within their setting who were doorways that could be flipped open to significant numbers of people, among whom a new church could be established.

A small core of believers is won to Christ and remains in a village. There they are baptized in the presence of all those who are not yet Christian, and there they publicly display the love which Christ shows them by the way in which they care for one another. In this natural setting, their friends and relatives see the powerful, supernatural transformation that Christ has made in their lives. The church grows rapidly. The quickest and most effective way to reach a nation for Christ is through the rapid planting of a multitude of small churches.

Chapter Seventeen: Do It Christ's Way, Not Our Way Luke 10

An excellent example of the application of Luke 10 may be found among the Chinese Christians. Just prior to the communist takeover in China, the Protestant church numbered less than one million members and was stagnant, depending upon the West for approximately ninety per cent of its finances. The door to Western funding and Western missionaries was shut in 1947. By 1966, at the end of the Cultural Revolution, the church was destroyed organizationally, and the believers purged.

A handful of Chinese believers followed Christ's methodology found in Luke 10. Within a matter of twenty-five years, the greatest burst of Christianity in the history of the church swept across China as an estimated 50,000,000 people were born again, baptized and gathered into 300,000 congregations and house churches! There are fourteen universal principles from Luke 10, on which evangelism methods should be built.

Work in Teams

After this the Lord appointed seventy-two others and sent them two by two (Luke 10:1). No army requires soldiers to fight alone! When troops are sent to battle, they are sent in squadrons or platoons; they are grouped together. They need each other for both encouragement and protection against the enemy. There is a popular slogan in Western evangelism, *Each One Reach One*. It is an expression of individualized evangelism. It teaches that if each Christian witnesses to one other person, we can win the world to Christ very quickly. While this idea may appeal mathematically, it does not work! The fact is that this slogan, *Each One Reach One,* is actually contrary to Christ's plan for evangelism.

He never sent the disciples out alone, but always in teams, for he realized that he was sending them out into serious spiritual warfare. They would need to counsel and direct each other, pray for each other, encourage each other, and minister to each other when they became spiritually wounded. *Each One Reach One* is a product of Western individualism and does not come from Scripture.

Acts 15:36 records the first serious quarrel in missions. Paul and Barnabas could not agree on the personnel for the mission team for the second missionary journey. The matter of team missions and the selection of candidates for the team was so serious that Barnabas and Paul split up over it. Barnabas chose John Mark and Paul chose Silas. God intervened, and won the victory, in that two teams went out, rather than one!

When Peter visited Cornelius, he did not go alone. *These six brothers also went with me and we entered the house* (Acts 11:12). Throughout all the records of the New Testament, we find that the Christians worked in groups, rather than following the *Each One Reach One* method. The Chinese Christians followed this example when, beginning in the mid-sixties, they systematically sent out teams of two people to reach the various villages.

Go Under Appointment

After this the Lord ***appointed*** *seventy- two* (Luke 10:1). This little statement, *The Lord appointed* is critical in implementing the proper methodology to reach a nation for Christ. Many Christians attempt to mobilize the entire church for evangelism. These efforts bear little fruit. Christ appointed seventy-two; he did not send everyone, but instead he selected certain ones for this task and gave them a special commission. This does not mean that Christians need not witness. All believers must be ready to explain their faith to anyone who asks for such an explanation. However, not all Christians are experts in the field of leading others to Christ, and our Lord tells us to select those whom he has specially gifted for that task, commission them, and send them out.

William Carey recognized this principle of missions. He saw that the church had to select a certain few and send them out in teams to reach specific areas for Christ. In the years that followed the formation of his mission society, a multitude of other mission societies quickly sprang up to commission specialists to go out in teams to reach others for Christ. It is due to our commitment to this principle of going out under appointment that Mission India grants the Institutes of Community Transformation only to churches. The schools are not open to individual Christians who want to enter one-by-one. The church is the basis for evangelism, and the church must appoint its evangelists and church planters and send them out.

Go Systematically

After this the Lord appointed seventy-two others and sent them two by two ahead of him to every town and place where he was about to go (Luke 10:1). A third principle upon which a mission vision should be built is that evangelism must be systematic and planned. It must be intentional; it must have an overall goal. When Christ sent out the seventy-two, he did not send them in a random way, to reach whoever might come in their path. He had a specific purpose that could be measured and accomplished, namely, to visit every village and town that he was going to enter.

In a private conversation with Dr. Donald McGavran several years ago, he stated that evangelism always had to be intentional. By this, he meant that evangelism, or the spread of the gospel, does not just happen. In his study of the subject, he found few instances where the gospel spread apart from the conscious sending and commissioning of specialists. This does not remove the privilege of witnessing and sharing Christ from all believers, but it does take a tremendous amount of guilt away from

Christians who are not necessarily gifted for bringing people to Christ. While our Lord told us that it is necessary for all to witness all the time, the advance of the gospel will come through teams of specialists, appointed by the church, and sent out to employ a systematic and measurable plan.

Go Into War

Go! I am sending you out like lambs among wolves (Luke 10:3). The more the church and its missionaries are aware that evangelism is a spiritual battle, the more equipped they will be to withstand the inevitable difficulties and perils of the task. The powers of darkness have claimed vast areas, and they will not surrender them easily. When Christ tells the seventy-two that he is sending them out as lambs among wolves, he warns them that they are no match for the demonic powers that they face. They are as helpless as a lamb facing a wolf. Every team that is commissioned to reach specific villages for Christ must go with the attitude that in themselves they are defenseless. Christ did not say this, however, to make them cringe. He said this in order to guide them to fix their eyes upon him. Just as Peter sank in the storm-tossed waters of the Sea of Galilee when he took his eyes from Christ, so certainly will a team sink when its eyes are taken from Christ. We are no more able, in our own strength, to stand against the devil than we are to walk on water. Every team must go in the supernatural strength of our precious Savior. This supernatural strength is important in all nations. There is no nation, including the Western countries, that is free from spiritual warfare.

Go Dependently

Do not take a purse or bag or sandals (Luke 10:4). One of the greatest obstacles to the spread of Christianity is money—too much money, not a lack of it! Christ not only advises us not to depend upon our own power in facing the demonic kingdom, when he tells us that we are like lambs among wolves, but he also prevents us from depending upon our money or the money of another country, when he tells us not to take any purse or bag or sandals.

How do we apply this principle to our situation in India? Simply put, the sooner the spread of the gospel is financed exclusively from India sources, the faster the gospel will spread throughout our country. William Carey saw and practiced this principle. When Carey formed the first mission society, he did not have in mind that this society would finance him for his entire life, but rather that this society would commission him, and furnish him with prayer support to get him started. He intended to make his mission team self-supporting, so that he could very rapidly draw funds from the work they would do in India. Carey was amazingly successful in this area, receiving only 600 pounds from his mission society, and generating 40,000 pounds for his mission through his own work in India. When mission leaders were asked at a Mission India conference, which churches were growing fastest in India, they answered, "Those which are not receiving foreign finance!"

Be Focused

And do not greet anyone on the road (Luke 10:4). One of the greatest weapons the devil has used to hinder the spread of the gospel is drawing our attention away from the goal and spreading us out in a variety of other excellent tasks, but tasks that do not accomplish that for which we are sent. He gets us to focus on what we want to do, to the elimination of focusing on what God calls us to do. The history of missions in India demonstrates this. Missions were started by Western Christians for the specific purpose of establishing churches. They quickly lost focus, however, and became engaged in a wide variety of excellent activities, all of which drained energy and power from their real calling.

Dr. McGavran's life changed when he met a servant on his mission compound who had worked faithfully for the mission for several years. He was curious about why she was not yet a Christian, and in response to his question, she replied that no one had ever explained Christianity to her! This shocked him as he realized that his mission was doing everything except the heart of its call, namely, to share Christ with those who had never heard! When Christ tells us not to greet anyone on the road, he is not instructing us to be rude, but rather to keep our focus. We must keep our focus clear—God has called us to plant clusters of disciples in every single area of India! Let nothing distract us from that task. We must always be aware that Satan's main tool is to tempt us to do the good God has not called us to do.

Target Homes

When you enter a house, first say, "Peace to this house" (Luke 10:5). Individuals are not our target, we are to target entire families and homes. We are to talk to families. We are to attempt to reach entire families. God has created us to live in community, and these natural communities of families must be the focus of our attempt to spread Christianity. Christ does warn us that there will be times when families are split over him, but this warning does not mean that we destroy families or tribes, but rather that we recognize them as God-given, and attempt to bring redemption to them, as well as to individuals.

Look For Persons of Peace

If a man of peace is there, your peace will be on him (Luke 10:6). Christ has special people in villages and towns who are persons of peace, or God seekers. These people, while not yet Christians, have had the Spirit of God working in their hearts prior to the arrival of the evangelist and have been prepared for this moment. Christ tells the seventy-two that if they cannot find such a person, they must move on to the next village. *But when you enter a town and are not welcomed, go into its streets and say, "Even the dust of your town we wipe from our feet as a warning to you"* (Luke 10:10-11). While this statement may seem severe, it is in keeping with Christ's command that they be focused. They are not to talk to people along the way, or waste time with non-receptive people. They are to search diligently for the persons of peace, the people in whose heart the Spirit of God has done preparatory work. It is their task to find these people as quickly as possible. This is God's mission vision! It is, of course, precisely here that evangelists become so discouraged. Christ warns us that there will be homes where no person has been prepared for the gospel prior to the arrival of the evangelist.

Ask for Help From Those You Reach

Stay there, eating and drinking whatever they give you, for the worker deserves his wages. When you enter a town and are welcomed, eat what is offered to you (Luke 10:7, 8). This is an extremely important point! One of the first things some Christians do upon coming into a village or neighborhood is to imply by their handouts that the nationals are not able to pay for the gospel but are instead financially dependent upon the missionary. Nothing cripples the spread of the gospel more rapidly than this insidious teaching. Roland Allen comments on this, "That one church should depend upon another for the supply of its ordinary expenses as a church, or even for a part of them, would have seemed incredible to the apostles." (*Mission Methods. St. Paul's or Ours?* Eerdmans, 1979, pg. 52.)

In the book of Acts, every new church was completely self-supporting from the beginning, so much so that they fed and cared for the missionaries from the moment they arrived in the village. Allen continues, "From this apostolic practice we are now as far removed in action as we are in time. We have indeed established here and there churches which support their own financial burdens, but for the most part our missions look to us for very substantial support." (*Mission Methods. St. Paul's or Ours?* Eerdmans, 1979, pg. 52.)

In China, the evangelists are sent out without food, and they have to find a man of peace in order to eat! There is a tremendous urgency created for the spread of the gospel, when, in order to eat, the evangelist must find a person of peace! The Chinese evangelists were taken into homes and were fed as they shared the gospel with the family. Very quickly, friends and relatives swarmed into the evening meetings, and usually within a matter of two weeks, a new cluster of believers was formed.

One of the greatest favors we can do for another person is to ask for his help! Christ practiced this approach with the Samaritan woman in John 4. He did not come to her and tell her that he had a better way to draw water, or that he had money for a new well. Rather, his approach was one of asking her for a favor. He, a Jew, asked a Samaritan woman for a drink of water! What Christ did in this act was to humble himself and place himself on her level so that communication could flow. Christians have ignored and violated this principle to the great detriment of the spread of Christianity. We have taught that the spread of the gospel throughout a nation must depend upon sources other than those of the converts! Christ tells us that even prior to conversion, the inquirers, and later the converts, must provide food for the missionaries!

Stay In One Home; Don't Move About

Do not move around from house to house (Luke 10:7). Why did Christ give this strange command? Would it not be better to continue to move about the village? Would it not be advisable to start as many Bible studies as possible? Perhaps it would, and one must be cautious in interpreting and adapting this principle to our methodology. Certainly, we are called to contact as many people as we can. What Christ had in mind, however, was the building of a cell or cluster of believers, and this can only be done in one location. We may begin with a number of family Bible studies, but it is best if we bring these studies together for regular worship in one home, preferably the home of a leader in the village. All should come to a central home for prayer and Bible study from the outset.

Minister to Physical Needs

Heal the sick (Luke 10:9). As we bring the gospel, it must touch all aspects of life and not be limited only to the spiritual. The gospel is racing through the villages of India, because the Spirit of God works in demonstrations of power by the healing of the sick and the casting out of demons. Apart from confrontation with demonic beings, Christians would have little opportunity to explain Christianity.

A striking example of this was a tribal group that experienced many miracles. A high caste couple lived near and heard stories of what was happening among the tribal people. The wife, who had been sick for twenty years, pleaded with her husband to pray to the God of the tribal people. The husband objected. Never would he lower himself to go to the untouchables and ask them to pray for his wife. However, wifely persuasion is a universal power, and she prevailed. The husband went to the river, looked across it at the untouchable's hut where their strange God, Jesus, was reportedly healing people, and he prayed, "God, whoever you are, you have been healing the untouchables. Can you show yourself and heal my wife also?" He returned home and found his wife miraculously and totally healed. Together, they raced over the river to the home where they knew people were praying to this strange new God called Jesus. They broke into the meeting, much to the surprise of the tribal people who had never had a high-caste Hindu visit their home. The high-caste couple asked about the name of the God who was healing people, and the tribal people told them his name was Jesus; they explained that he brought both spiritual and physical healing. The couple was introduced to Jesus, and they gave their lives to him.

The tribal people then informed the couple that they had been in fervent prayer for the high-caste community; knowing that the high-caste community would never listen to a tribal, they had been praying that Jesus would heal a high-caste person and send that person back to the high-caste community. They told this couple that they were now commissioned to bring the Good News to their high-caste neighbors, since they would never listen to an untouchable tribal. Soon, the high-caste community across the river formed a new church.

Go in God's Authority

Whoever listens to you listens to me; he who rejects you rejects me; but he who rejects me rejects him who sent me... He (Jesus) replied, "I saw Satan fall like lightning from heaven. I have given you authority . . . to overcome all the power of the enemy" (Luke 10:16, 18). One of the great problems of the Western Christian is his failure to understand the authority that Christ has given him and to use that authority properly over the demonic. When we confront the world of evil in our own power, we are like lambs among wolves; but, when we do so in the power of Christ, we are like lions among mice.

Leave As Quickly As You Can

There is no specific text on which this principle can be built, but there is a sense of urgency and movement within these instructions of Christ. The seventy-two are not to take up permanent residence in these homes but are to be there only temporarily. Missionaries often stay too long, so the new converts become dependent upon them, and this cripples them. The apostle Paul carried out most of his work within ten years, four of which he spent in prison! I am certain that he wanted to stay longer in many of the cities he visited, but God allowed persecution to come in virtually every place, and this forced Paul and the team to move on, leaving behind a small cluster of new believers.

Keep a Clear Goal In Mind

Finally, we need to keep in mind that our task is to form self-governing, self-multiplying, self-financing clusters of new believers in every village and people group throughout India. It is a tremendous task. We need to establish specific, local goals for each district and state. We then need to pull these goals together into a national goal. Christians must work together to accomplish this with a new sense of urgency.

God's Mission Vision

Chapter Eighteen: Don't Stifle Evangelism with Education

The relationship of Christianity to education is this: A Christian cannot live without education, nor can he or she live with too much education. India needs schools and education. Over half of India's population is partially or fully illiterate. However, India also has an abundance of Christian institutions of higher learning. Many of the Indian Christian leaders are very well educated; many hold multiple degrees. But, is the surge to complete the Great Commission originating with the educated or with those who lack the degrees? There is no question that new converts need education and training. Mission India's main purpose is to provide training and education to reach the goal of completing the Great Commission. But, there are important questions and reservations about education that we must always keep in mind. Both church and college are set up to produce *hearers*, rather than *doers*. Apprenticeship is not part of Christian education. Much of what the students *do* does not relate to practical life.

Dr. George Patterson was a missionary in Honduras, associated with the Honduras Bible Institute for several years. For many years, he taught a course in church planting to the national Christians without much success. He taught the course in the normal manner— give the class notes and lectures, and then administer tests. He then expected the students to go out and *do it*, but very little was done. The students seemed to have the idea that just listening to the lectures and passing the tests was all that was required of them!

Mr. Patterson then restructured his teaching. He refused to teach more than one or two lessons in a row without the students putting the lesson into practice. They were given specific practical goals that they had to meet before they could go on to study the next lesson. This change revolutionized education, for now the practice was mixed in with the principle; students actually did what they were taught to do! Very quickly, dozens of new churches were planted where previously, virtually no church planting activity had occurred.

Mr. Patterson developed his theory regarding the education of new converts even further. Rather than educating them first in doctrine, he believed that they should first be educated in obedience. New Christians should first learn how to give, how to pray, and how to worship. After they learn these things, they should start *to do* what they have learned. One can study all the principles associated with playing a musical instrument, but until one starts to play, one will never master the instrument!

Education is not an up-front, priority matter. When we first educate the new convert before he evangelizes, we mislead the new convert to believe that unless we educate him, he is unable to reach others for Christ. Rather upon conversion, he should turn outward, not inward, and go to the other members of his family and village to share what has happened to him. The man born blind whom Jesus healed needed no special training to testify to the Pharisees that he was once blind but could now see, and that Jesus was the one who healed him!

Allen says: The spread of the gospel…is "hindered by a very widespread conviction amongst our missionaries that new converts, so far from evangelizing others, need to be nursed themselves if they are not to fall away. We often hear some such expression as this: Even after baptism, the new life in Christ must be carefully tended or inevitably the first fervor will cool and the early enthusiasm will be quenched by the deadly heathenism all around. That is a voice which teaches that the way to retain the consciousness of a gift received is not by handing it on to others, but by learning to depend more and more on teachers." (*Spontaneous Expansion*, pg. 32.)

Not only does the introduction of education at too early a point in training give the new convert the idea that he need not hand on his gift to others, but it also teaches him that he is dependent upon the missionary and teacher and can do little without him. Thus, we have made two tragic mistakes through the early introduction of education. We have taught the new convert that he must look inward to himself first, rather than out to the other non-Christian families and friends. He must depend on the missionary/teacher rather than upon the Holy Spirit and the Word.

The Pentecostal churches of Latin and South America have a practice of not admitting any person to their seminaries that has not planted a church and pastored it for five years. This practical proof that he is gifted is the evidence needed for admission to higher education. Having had his personality set in an outward-looking direction for these five years of church planting and pastoring, the student is not likely to be ruined and turned from soul-orientation to degree-orientation by his experience in seminary.

Some of the Mission India church planting students are graduates of Bible Schools and seminaries, and these students testify that they learned far more Bible in the trimester church planter program than in their academic programs. Mission India has adopted three simple steps in education: *learn it, do it, and report it*. We have the choice between two methods of education. In one, the student retains 10% of what he learns; in the other, he retains 90% of what he learns. We immediately react by stating that we wish to use the 90%-method. The fact is, however, that Christians use the 10%-method most of the time! We need to learn how to guide people in discovering the truths of Scripture and sharing it with others. As they discover, implement, and share, the truth of Scripture will enter their mind in a powerful, lasting way.

In addition to stifling evangelism with education and plucking people out of their potential mission field and plopping them in church where they are sterilized within a short period, we do not have a clear definition of the Great Commission; hence, we have little idea of what progress we have made toward fulfilling it. We have wandered far from the methodology of evangelism that our Savior demonstrated.

Chapter Nineteen; Don't Cripple Converts with Cash

We have hindered the spread of the gospel by making converts dependent upon our money. If these fundamental mistakes are corrected, and outreach is conducted according to God's Mission Vision, amazing results occur. Instead of substituting the good we want to do for the good God calls us to do, let us humbly wait on him to lead us into his Mission Vision, namely the spontaneous spread of the Good News in Christ.

Money is like fertilizer. Fertilizer, wisely and sparingly used, helps crops grow, but when applied in large amounts, the very thing that made the crops grow, kills them. Money and missions are related in the same way as fertilizer and crops are related. Money is needed for missions, but too much money, wrongly applied, kills missions more quickly, more effectively and more certainly than any other single factor.

One of the most important factors hindering the spread of the gospel today is not persecution or resistance to the gospel, but it is the wrong use of finance. Roland Allen summarized it in these pointed words: "How can a man propagate a religion which he cannot support, and which he cannot expect those whom he addresses to be able to support?" (Allen, *Spontaneous Expansion*, Eerdmans, pg. 35.) In other words, if the religion is not worth financing, it is worth little at all. Believers in India must ask themselves: "Why is it that a country, such as India, can find all the funds needed to erect massive temples and mosques, and yet when people turn to Christianity, we suddenly seem to be so poor that we need others to help us financially? If we are able to build our own Hindu temples and Muslim mosques, why do we need help in building our church buildings?"

Several years ago, when it first started schools of evangelism, Mission India trained ten men who were recent converts to Christianity to plant churches. As with most new converts, the men proved to be excellent church planters, and they experienced great results. However, when the Western Christians who gave them money for their training visited them, the church planters told these Christians how poor they were. They said that they could not carry on without continuing financial aid. When this was reported to a supervisor, he asked them the following questions.

"Did you drink before conversion?"

"Yes", they all replied.

"Do you drink now?"

"No," was their answer.

"Did you gamble before becoming a Christian?"

"Oh, yes, sir," they all replied.

"Do you gamble now?"

"Oh no, sir, that is not what a Christian should do!"

"Did you attend the cinemas before conversion?"

"Yes, we did," they replied.

"And, do you go now?"

"Oh no, sir!"

"Did you smoke before becoming Christians?"

"Yes, sir!"

“Do you smoke now?”

“No, sir!”

The examiner continued. “This is amazing. Before you became Christians, you had plenty of money to spend on drinking, smoking, gambling, and the cinema. Now that you have become Christians, you do not spend money on these things any more. Here are four areas in which you are saving money. Why did you pretend to those foreigners that you were so poor that you had to have money from them? Have you no pride? If you could get along before this and waste all that money, why, after becoming a Christian and saving all this money, do you now need foreign assistance?” The men were shamed by the questions and wrote to those who had so generously sponsored them in the school, “Praise God! He is now supplying all our needs, and we do not need any more help!”

In another area of the country, Mission India trained ten church planters among very poor tribal people. Five substantial churches sprang up, but because the people were so poor, they were churches without buildings. In one village, the elders rolled out a rug for worship, and the Christians sat on it as they praised God. This was their church. Since they did not have a suitable place for worship, some well-meaning, generous foreigners gave them a gift of money that, although it seemed quite a small gift to the foreigners, was far beyond anything the villagers had ever received before. They were unable to handle so much money, and the elders of the church began to quarrel among themselves over its use, with the result that the gift was never used to build a church building. Tragically, there was no need for a church building after the gift, for the quarreling and disunity that resulted killed the little church.

Peter was a poor fisherman turned church planter. He had done well. He had planted a number of new churches among the fishing villages, but then he was expelled from his own village by the elders, and the new churches underwent severe persecution. Everything he had done was in danger of collapsing. As we visited, my heart was touched, and when he asked for a gift of money to buy a new boat, I was reaching for my wallet to give it to him; immediately, unexpected words came out of my mouth: "Peter, I never give money for boats. What I will do is to get a number of people to pray that God will give you the funds for the boat."

I looked around and wondered where those words had come from. When I realized I had spoken them, I felt that I was the biggest hypocrite in India at that moment. I was miserable. It is so much easier to give than not to give, especially when you have the money.

I told his story at one of MI's largest funding banquets, and I asked the donors to pray for Peter. As the year went by, I forgot about Peter and the prayer request. I went back to India a year later to speak at a conference of church planters. Peter was sitting in the front row.

I could hardly wait to finish speaking. I greeted Peter and eagerly asked if he had gotten his new boat. He looked at me with a questioning look. He seemed to be saying, "Didn't you pray as you promised?" He didn't say that. He said, "Yes, God answered your prayers and provided a new boat." I rejoiced and asked forgiveness from God for doubting my own advice. I asked Peter how he had done that year, since he could now finance himself with his new boat. He replied that it had gone fairly well; he had planted nine new churches!

A missionary to South America told me that he, too, was working among tribal people who were so poor that they had no cash. Christianity spread rapidly among the people, and after about fifty of them were baptized, they expressed a desire to have a church building. Since they had no money, they asked the missionary to go to his country and raise funds so that they could build a building. The missionary gently refused. "God is great," he said. "He has healed many sicknesses in this village.

He has shown his power over demons. He has saved many. If he has done these great things, then it is a small thing for him to provide the finances needed to build a church building, if this is what he wants. I counsel you to fast and pray for thirty days, asking God to provide the money so you can build a church building. If, after that time, the funds have not yet arrived, I will ask my friends from abroad to help with the building."

The tribe fasted and prayed. Each year they had raised a small crop of carrots and sold them. The proceeds never amounted to much money, but it was all they received all year. That year, after fasting and praying, they experienced a tremendous harvest of carrots, and the price they received for their sale mysteriously was far, far greater than anything they had ever experienced. They had enough money for a new church building. They didn't have to ask for funds! God will provide the funds. Christians within a country need only build upon the financial level that is accepted within that country; this is the level that everyone can afford. We need not import economic standards and building designs from other countries, attractive as these buildings may be, for they will hinder the spread of the gospel, rather than help it.

Roland Allen makes an excellent point of the fact that no nation can finance the spread of the gospel in another nation!

Not only is such a thing not feasible, financially, but it will make the gospel odorous within the receiving nation. Even if the supply of men and funds from Western sources was unlimited and we could cover the whole globe with an army of millions of foreign missionaries and establish mission stations thickly all over the world, the method would speedily reveal its weakness, as it already is beginning to reveal it.

The mere fact that Christianity was propagated by such an army, established in foreign stations all over the world, would inevitably alienate the native populations, who would see in it the growth of the domination of a foreign people. They would see themselves robbed of their religious independence, and would more and more fear the loss of their social independence. Foreigners can never successfully direct the propagation of any faith throughout a country. If the faith does not become naturalized and expand among the people by its own vital power, it exercises an alarming and hateful influence, and men fear and shun it as something alien. It is then obvious that no sound missionary policy can be based upon multiplication of missionaries and mission stations. A thousand thousand would not suffice; a dozen might be too many. (Ibid pg.19)

As long as Christians look outside their nation to others to finance the spread of the gospel, Christianity will be hindered in its flow into every people group and village! God is not waiting for foreigners to give generously so that India may be reached; he is waiting for Indian Christians to look to him, rather than to others to fund their needs in his own miraculous way.

One of the most startling examples of mission finance is the explosion of the church in China. In 1947, when the communists shut the doors to all Western mission activity in China, the Protestant church was stagnant, non-witnessing, and dependent upon Western Christians for ninety percent of all its financing! Here is a classic case of crippling converts with cash. Through unrestrained generosity, the Western missionaries had effectively taught the Chinese Christian that unless Western finance was available, they were too poor to reach their own nation with the gospel! As long as they were depending upon Western finance, the church in China did not grow. When the communists took over, and all missionaries were expelled and foreign financing stopped, people thought that the church in China was dead. Without missionaries to teach and train, and without the money from the West, the church could not last. Little did they realize that, while these were necessary ingredients to establish the church in China, they had now become the greatest obstacles to the spread of Christianity. The church did collapse under communism; by the end of the Cultural Revolution, very little was left of the ecclesiastical structure. However, the faith of the Chinese Christians burned more brightly than ever.

Without any training from the West, or without any Western financing, God worked in these Chinese Christians to bring about a massive spread of the gospel. Today, there are an estimated three hundred thousand congregations, filled with more than an estimated one hundred million vibrant new believers, and all of it is financed within the country! The nationals need to rethink their position! Both pragmatic and principle arguments militate against the spread of the gospel in a nation when it is based on foreign financing. Roland Allen rightly states,

And as for self-extension, it is surely plain that a church which could neither support itself nor govern itself could not multiply itself. For a long time men thought (self-support) was impossible; they declared that the poverty of their converts was so profound that to expect them to provide the material for common religious life was absurd and many of our missionaries still say the same today. But that self-support from the very beginning is possible has been abundantly proved, not in rare sporadic instances, but by the wider experience of those missionaries who set themselves to encourage the evangelization of the country by their converts from the very beginning....Nothing is so weakening as the habit of depending upon others for those things which we ought to supply for ourselves. Nothing more undermines the spirit which should express itself in spontaneous activity. (*Ibid* pp. 27, 34, 35.)

Mission India has developed the following financial guidelines, which are an attempt to set the Indian church free from financial dependency. We are convinced that until that happens, the church will never be able to reach this nation for Christ.

Never Give Anything For Free!

Christ's specific command to the seventy-two (Luke 10:7) is violated repeatedly in missions today. Christ implies that the convert should provide food for those who bring the gospel from the very outset. One of our church planter students desired to plant a church in a slum area of a well-known southern city. When he entered the slum, people asked him what he was bringing—water, health programs, etc.? When he replied that he was bringing only the good news about Jesus Christ, they would not listen to him. They had become so hardened and calloused by the free handouts of mission organizations that they had become deaf to the gospel. They were interested only in the money that missions offered.

This student did not give up, but remained in the village, living among the people. Finally, someone who was impressed with the man's tenacity became curious about his message, so he started a small Bible study in his home, which then grew into a substantial church. The student, under Mission India guidelines, even refused to give any Scriptures or tracts away in the village; instead, he made the inquirers pay a small amount of money for everything he gave them.

Mission India's policy, from the outset, has been to charge a minimal amount for all Scripture. This fee should be small enough that it does not hinder even the poorest from obtaining the Scripture if they truly want it. The cost, however, is always above waste paper value, which keeps it from being sold as refuse. Charging the small fee places a value on the material.

A young communist purchased a Scripture packet for half of a rupee, or about eight cents. He was attracted by the colorful cover of the *Guide to Happiness* course and its low price. When he got home and discovered that it was Christian literature, he threw it on the table, but he did not throw it away, for he had paid for it! The materials lay on the table for a few months; then his younger brother picked them up and read them. He was fascinated by what he read, and although he was a communist, he decided that he wanted to distribute this material. He ordered several thousand copies, and he and his friends began to distribute the course. Only after the second order came in, did the MI representatives go to the area to investigate. They introduced these people to Christ, and a small church was formed. Had the materials merely been given away, there would have been no value placed upon them, and they would have been destroyed.

Never Do For a Convert What He Can Do For Himself

Charles Brock was a church planter in the Philippines for many years, and from his experience wrote, *The Principles and Practice of Indigenous Church Planting*. In this book, he writes that everything a church planter does in a church should be done so that the church can reproduce itself. The way a church is born will influence its ability to reproduce itself. A church planter cannot be sure every church he plants will actually begin new churches, but he can do everything possible to leave the way open for self-reproducing church life. A church's view of reproduction will be learned early.

Every action of the church planter becomes part of a lesson learned by the church, even during its birth. If the church planter is fully aware of the need for thinking that everything that is done must be reproducible, he will be more likely to plant a church that is capable of reproduction. Thus, the church planter should immediately allow the new converts to lead their own worship service, guiding them as he would his own children, to do things themselves, rather than doing those things for them. Every attempt must be made to avoid all forms of dependency by the new converts on the missionary.

Never Give a New Convert a Technique for Evangelism Which He Cannot Reproduce

A marketing survey was carried out by some major corporations in India to determine the best way to communicate with the thousands of villages. They attempted to determine the effectiveness of radio, video, the printed page, and cassettes. Much to their amazement, they found none of the above to be very effective; instead, they learned that the age-old technique of using drama and plays was by far the most effective means. Hence, some corporations have discarded modern methods, and are advertising in the villages through the more musical means of drama. This is an effective method of communication, economically reproducible by villagers, and one with which they are completely comfortable. While it may not be the most effective method of communication by urban standards, we are not trying to reach urban people, but rather village people.

Never Imply That the Spread of Christianity Throughout the Nation Depends on Foreign Financing

All foreign financing should be kept out of the establishment of new churches, if they are going to reproduce themselves throughout the nation. Nothing will halt the spread of Christianity more effectively than teaching the new converts that they are too poor to spread the gospel and need outside help! It is the single most damaging and most inhibiting factor in the spread of the gospel. Instead of traveling to other countries, attempting to raise funds for national evangelists, only to pay them a pittance each month, it would be far better to travel through our more well-established churches in India, teaching principles of stewardship and raising funds within our own nation. All foreign funding must be secondary funding. It should never be administered to the actual pastors, church planters, or their buildings. The funding should be used behind the scenes; it should be discreet, designed to enable the mission and the church to fund itself.

Teach the new convert that the quickest way out of poverty is through giving (2 Corinthians 9:10).

God has given a promise. *Now he who supplies seed to the sower and bread for food will also supply and increase your store of seed and will enlarge the harvest of your righteousness* (2 Corinthians 9:10). Enlarging your store of seed means that God will increase the ability of those who give to give more! Thus, if we wish to be delivered from poverty so that we can give more to the Lord, we must take the first step by giving to the Lord. Introduce faith-promise giving. In faith-promise giving, a Christian makes a private, personal commitment to ask God for a sum of money for missions, above that which he can afford to give on his own. He prays daily for that money and asks God to supply those funds in a supernatural and unexpected way. Stories abound of God's amazing provision!

A woman made a covenant with God that for thirty days she would give God anything extra that he sent into her life. Midway through that month, she received a letter with a check for twenty thousand rupees! The writer of the letter said that he had borrowed this amount from her parents several years ago and had never repaid it. During the course of the month, he had felt a strange urge to repay the amount, and learning that her parents were dead, he sent the check to her as their only living relative!

God is working throughout the villages of India in amazing ways. Stories of healings and exorcisms abound. God who can heal the sick and cast out the demons is able to work miracles in the area of finance. Why can we not do more to trust him and challenge our people to give? The Bible mentions giving some five hundred times, while it mentions prayer only three hundred times! It is amazing that Paul holds up one of the poorest churches of the New Testament era as the model of a generous church: *And now, brothers and sisters, we want you to know about the grace that God has given the Macedonian churches. In the midst of a very severe trial, their overflowing joy and their extreme poverty welled up in rich generosity* (2 Corinthians 8:1-2).

Paul says that the extreme poverty of the Macedonian church was one of the main motivations for it to give! One of the poorest churches in the world gave to a church that had been one of the richest churches but had come on hard times. It would be similar to the churches of India taking collections for the churches in the West! Poverty did not keep the Macedonian church from giving; rather, it was one of their motivations to give. Perhaps the fresh pain of knowing the suffering of poverty brought about a tender love and compassion for others who were going through difficult times. Perhaps the lack of material gifts made it easier to give the little that they had. It is the rich that find it most difficult to be separated from their many possessions!

We must learn the lessons of mission finance as taught by the Scriptures. Foreign financing will never be the means for reaching India for Christ! Indian churches, in keeping with their economic ability, must carry out the spread of the gospel. This will release untold energy and take away the great mental block of thinking, *we are poor*, which so hinders mission work. New believers will know that they shall see every nation, tribe, people group and language in heaven, for this is God's Mission Vision.

Epilogue

We received the following story via email from India. With tears in his eyes, Paul described the graduation celebration of church planters in his county (India).

We cannot stop people from coming to the celebration. We told each (new) church to bring only 8-10 people, but they just keep coming. Auto-rickshaws that may only carry six passengers were loaded with 12. And so many new believers were there, so many testimonies...I never saw such fruit in my life.

We started with a small fellowship in a rural area. I trained my team of leaders in a Bible College way for two years. Working together, they planted only one church in five years. But, after the Mission India church planter training program, every one of them became a church planter, and each person has planted more than three churches. It has not stopped. Their leaders now are also planting churches.

They are going to **so** *many places. One of the church planters came to me after some time. He began work in a new town. He said, "Pastor Paul, you have to come to my place where we are opening a new church building." I went and saw that he had a 4-wheeler. I asked him where it came from, and he said, "We are planting so many churches we needed a vehicle, so that we can go along and help with the new churches."*

These workers who are trained have many blessings. Not only saving souls, but also they are good leaders and train new believers to plant churches and train new leaders. So many thousands now are being baptized. Almost 35,000 have been baptized in this county in the last three years!

Praise God for His Mission Vision!

From author John DeVries

Why Give?

In this 40-day devotional, author John DeVries tells us that Christians were meant to be life-giving rivers, not stagnant ponds. Five profound reasons are given to help Christians experience the joy of giving. Offer your church a 5-week journey through the Why Give? book. Available through www.reachingamerica.net or through Amazon.

Check out the Reaching America web site bookstore for Why Give? resources and free down-loads to lead your church through a special time of stewardship renewal.

The
Experience
of Waiting,
unning, and
Walking
A Study of the Book of Acts